HOW TO BUILD
A LONG-LASTING FIRE

HOW TO BUILD
A LONG-LASTING FIRE
Writing Poems from Your Life

Carol Morrison

NTC *Publishing Group*
Lincolnwood, Illinois USA

This book is for Aaron.

Literary credits are to be found on page 229, which should be considered an extension of this copyright page.

Sponsoring Editor: Marisa L. L'Heureux
Cover design: Ophelia M. Chambliss
Interior design: Julie Anderson
Production Manager: Rosemary Dolinski

ISBN: 0-8442-5935-7 (student text)
ISBN: 0-8442-5936-5 (instructor's edition)

Library of Congress Cataloging-in-Publication Data

Morrison, Carol (Carol A.)
    How to build a long-lasting fire : writing poems from your life /
Carol Morrison.
        p.   cm.
    Includes index.
    ISBN 0-8442-5935-7 (pbk.)
    1. Poetry—Study and teaching (Secondary)   2. English language—
Composition and exercises.   3. Creative writing (Secondary
education)   4. Poetry—Authorship.   I. Title.
PN1101.M67   1996
808.1—dc20   96-2713
                                                                CIP

Published by NTC Publishing Group
© 1997 NTC Publishing Group, 4255 West Touhy Avenue
Lincolnwood (Chicago), Illinois 60646-1975 U.S.A.

67890 VL 987654321

CONTENTS

CHAPTER 6
FANNING THE FLAMES:
Revision   150

CHAPTER 7
TENDING THE FIRE:
Poems from Your Own Life   170

CHAPTER 8
MAINTAINING THE FIRE:
Poems from People, Places, and Things   198

PREFACE

This book is different from others you have used. It does not devote
chapter after chapter to "appreciating" poetry, and it does not treat
poetry as a puzzle that can be solved only by learning intricate analyti-
cal techniques. It is not written as a textbook. Instead, it is written as a
guidebook to help you light your own long-lasting fire—the fire of writing poetry.

This book is written to you in the same informal tone that I use with
my own students. My editor calls it "idiosyncratic." I call it "personal."
Poetry itself is personal. As the title of the book suggests, poetry comes
from inside you, from your own life. Since that is true, it seems to me
that the only way to learn about poetry is from the inside. You learn to
write poems by writing poems.

Right from the start, you will be writing every day, just as professional writers do. As you move from lesson to lesson, you will learn
ways to make your poems stronger. Since poetry is an art, you will
develop your technique through apprenticeship—the way art has been
learned for centuries. You will study models from successful poets in the
same way art students study the paintings of the masters. Some of these
models will be from professional poets, but most will be from students
just like you, students who were my partners in this book. Other poems
will be my own, since I cannot teach writing without writing myself.

While the lessons in this book can be followed sequentially by an
individual student, they are ideally intended for a workshop environ-
ment where you will find encouragement and support from other writers. Like others who have followed this approach, you will learn how to
build a long-lasting fire that will burn throughout your life and yield
poems. As you will come to see, poetry is a way of life.

Your opportunities for writing will be found throughout the book. They are called "Firestarters," and I hope they will do just that—light fires of inspiration for your writing. These exercises will give you the skills you need to get started, suggest leads that will result in poems, take you through approaches to revision, and show you how to find ideas for poems throughout your life.

Acknowledgments

Thank you to Lucien Stryk and Mort Castle for their encouragement and to Marisa L. L'Heureux for her editorial guidance.

CHAPTER 1

PREPARING FOR THE FIRE:

Getting Started

II Most people begin with no ash in the fireplace, and proceed to build the fire with paper and dry kindling wood laid directly on top of the andirons. This explodes into a large scary blaze. As soon as this dies down, so that one can get close enough to it, larger logs are thrown on top and another large uncontrollable blaze is quickly lived and dies out. All of this results in a fire constantly needing attention, either too hot or too cold, too large or too small. *II*

Raymond W. Dyer,
The Old Farmer's Almanac

WORKSHOPS: A Community of Writers

The University of Iowa Writers Workshop is generally credited with being the most popular writing workshop. Both the undergraduate and graduate writing programs at Iowa and most other universities use the workshop approach. At Iowa, classes are divided by genre: poetry workshops function separately from fiction workshops. However, at many smaller colleges and most high schools, the workshops include both genres. The important factor is not the genre under study; it is the opportunity for serious writers to interact with other serious writers.

You may have discovered already that your family and friends may not be the best audience for your work. In most cases they love you and are reluctant to criticize; in other cases they may be overly harsh because of unfamiliarity with the intent of the writing, and rarely are they deeply enough involved in writing to give you concrete suggestions. For these reasons it is important to work within a writing community, where the teacher operates more as guide and facilitator and where writers respond to each other's work with sensitivity and understanding. As the network of community develops, most writers find that the workshop helps them step outside of their work and view it objectively. My own students work together as a family, giving encouragement, ideas, suggestions, and even constructive criticism without injured feelings or resentment. In fact, after the first few months, the workshop operates with its own momentum; the students instinctively take their work to their trusted friends for comments and feedback. This is not surprising; this is how most professional writers work. They develop lines of deep rapport with other writers who then serve as their audience. Most of us have in mind two or three special individuals for whom we write, although ultimately we aim our work for a general audience. Your classroom workshop can help you establish mutually profitable friendships with other writers that may last a lifetime.

Your instructor will be instrumental in establishing the workshop atmosphere, but he or she will need help and cooperation from all the members. In a workshop the teacher does not serve as an authority or disciplinarian; therefore much greater responsibility is placed on each member. In some workshops the teacher sits in only as questioner and facilitator, allowing the students to find their own way to art. This method was promoted by the late William Stafford, who taught almost entirely through questioning the students. He trusted them ultimately to find their own answers, although the answers might be longer in coming. In other workshops, the teacher takes a role of greater leadership, much as Mark Strand practices with his students. Since he has far more background and experience in his art, he saves his students time in their apprenticeship through gentle but firm guidance early in their development. He is careful to be nurturing rather than prescriptive and to allow students to develop individual styles and voices. Teachers may lean toward either the Stafford or the Strand model, depending on their personalities and the composition of the class. They may even begin by asserting more guidance early in the year and loosening their approach as students become more practiced in their art.

Regardless of the approach your teacher decides to take, certain guidelines are essential for a successful workshop. Some hints drawn from my own experience are listed below; your class may decide to add others as you adapt to this approach:

1. Sit in a circle if at all possible. The teacher will be part of this circle. In this way all members are equal and all may maintain eye contact. Also, as one of my former students pointed out, it reflects the idea of revision: a circle that moves round and round.

2. Read the work aloud. This is especially important for poetry, where sound is such an important element. You will find that the ear can detect problems the eye overlooks. Also, the oral reading allows immediate participation from all members of the group. Ideally, you should provide photocopies or computer copies for each member, but a workshop can operate without them. If so, you may be asked to reread parts or all of the poem. If copies are not provided, jot down notes as the writer reads.

3. Never interrupt while someone is reading.

4. Every member must participate. For this reason the class may need to divide into smaller work groups. Some workshops work with as many as fifteen writers in the circle; however, I find that beginning writers seem more comfortable in groups of five or six. For some activities, we work as a whole class workshop, but at least initially, the smaller groups are more expedient for the critiquing process. Also, it is absolutely imperative that every member of the group fulfill all assignments. Nothing can kill a writing community faster than a self-designated authority who criticizes others but does no writing. Unless speakers prove themselves to be writers through the act of writing, they carry no credibility as critics. Equally deadly can be the member who never comments at all. Most beginning writers are self-conscious and interpret silence as disapproval. In the early weeks of a workshop it is helpful to require at least one comment from each member. Many

workshops designate one student each day as facilitator to ensure that everyone speaks. The facilitator then indicates which member will make the initial comments for each piece of work.

5. Begin with a general reaction rather than a minor point. Every writer wants to know the gut reaction of a reader.

6. Always offer a positive point before criticizing. Later, when members are comfortable with one another and certain of their own talent, they may choose to jump immediately into suggestions for revision. Many of my advanced students reach this point. They have worked together for more than two years and recognize that all are competent writers. They already know what is right with their work; now they wish to know what is wrong in order to grow as writers.

7. React to the writing rather than the subject. For example, most of us have been in love, but that doesn't mean that every poem about love is well written. Before critiquing early work, it is useful to list what specific points the group will look for in each assignment. It can be overwhelming and discouraging to react to everything. Like any art, the writing of poetry is cumulative and can be expected to spiral as it grows.

8. Be vigilant against clichés. Poetry depends on imagery; imagery depends on imagination. Clichés betray lapses in imagination.

9. Respect the voice and vision of others. One danger of the workshop approach is that a dominant member may unduly influence the others until everyone's poems sound the same.

Your workshop can become an organic entity that outlives its individual members. This is an ideal situation if you can manage it. To create a self-perpetuating workshop you will need to bring in members of various ages. This is possible in most high schools, where students can be involved from their freshman through senior years. The older students become role models and mentors for the younger students, who grow older and take their places. In our own workshop it is not at all unusual for college students and graduates to sit in for a class during their vacations or to act as workshop speakers and leaders during the year. Their willingness to stay involved has added a higher level of experience and professionalism to our program. As your own workshop grows, it will adapt itself to the needs and personalities of its members and become a living community of writers.

JOURNALS

At a recent writers' conference, a student asked the four professional authors who had just read from their work whether they "wrote down their ideas." The four writers smiled sheepishly, then began pulling from their pockets notebooks, paper, and more paper. The answer was obvious: yes, writers do write down their ideas. Some use formal journals; some small spiral notebooks; others scraps of paper that they later file or tape into larger notebooks. They have learned never to trust memory, that most fallible of human resources.

Poets go even a step further. They actively seek ideas; they train their senses to observe more acutely; they look for the question behind every answer; they take nothing, absolutely nothing, for granted. A few weeks ago, one of my students told me with great excitement that she had seen one of our country's most renown poets at a local shopping mall. "Do you mean he was actually carrying shopping bags ?" I asked. "Sort of," she said. "He was sitting in the food court with some bags at his feet and jotting notes furiously on a small spiral pad."

Every writer I know stops to record ideas whenever they occur. Sometimes writers may be fortunate enough to have a notepad with them; other times they may use a paper napkin or the back of a program. I have written entire poems on the backs of hall passes. Granted, it may require several hall passes, but the poem is there, on paper. Even more inconveniently, many writers find that most of their ideas come to them in that twilight state between consciousness and sleep. No doubt, this is because the subconscious is closer to the surface, that same subconscious that controls your dreams. Take my word for it: either keep paper and pen near your bed or force yourself to get up and write the idea on paper; if you do not, you will surely have forgotten it by morning. Nothing is worse than to have the memory of a wonderful idea, but absolutely no inkling of what that idea was! From years of experience, I can assure you that it is possible to write semilegibly in a nearly dark room and that the ideas will be worth recording. I often wake suddenly at two or three in the morning with an idea for a poem or story or writing lesson. I can only assume that my subconscious was at work on the problem while I slept and then awakened me with the solution.

At this point you probably agree that a writer's journal is a good idea, but you may be wondering just what to write in it. Let's begin by discussing what not to write. Rule #1: A journal is not a diary. A diary is a record of your day; a journal is a record of your ideas. Your journal is not an appropriate place for a litany of the events that made up your day. Here are some suggestions for experiments in your writer's journal:

1. Write a series of unfocused and focused freewritings. You may set aside ten minutes and write whatever comes to mind, or you may set out to write on a predetermined subject.

2. Record phrases, sentences, and stylistic tricks that please you as you read the work of others. Analyze what works.

3. Try emulating the styles of authors you admire, just for fun. Write a poem in the style of e. e. cummings, a descriptive paragraph like Ernest Hemingway, a nonfiction passage like Annie Dillard.

4. Create your own epigrams, parables, words of wisdom.

5. Practice any kind of sensory description: eating spaghetti, ice skating, swimming in the ocean, watching fireworks . . .

6. Record meticulously the most ordinary concrete details: the shape of your foot, a comparison of your index fingers, drinking hot chocolate on a cold morning, the lightning bugs in your backyard, the sound of a distant freight train in the night . . .

7. Collect characters by jotting down concrete details of people you see each day. These can be strangers you observe from a distance or family and friends closest to you.

8. Ask yourself questions and write out your answers.

9. Begin with a fact and look for the questions behind it.

10. Write a letter to yourself to be read five years from now.

11. Jot down images for poems to write in the future.

12. Write down comparisons, all kinds of comparisons. They are the backbone of poetry.

13. Practice writing figures of speech.

14. Accumulate several intuitive freewritings.

15. List topics that you would like to write about someday.

16. Write down any descriptive phrases, borrowed or original, that please you.

17. Practice any of the lessons contained in this book.

Perhaps the most reassuring way to look at your journal is as a place to take risks, even to fail; a place to collect whatever you wish, whenever you wish. The journal is yours; it is you, and it should not be graded. However, your teacher will read, comment on, and initial your entries each week.

A Potpourri of Journal Entries

Your journal will be as individual and distinctive as you are, but you may find it helpful to read some of the kinds of entries other students have written in their journals. Of course the original journal entries all included the dates on which they were written, but I am omitting dates here since they would be meaningless in such a smorgasbord:

There are several words that spawn teaming thoughts in my mind. "Belly" brings round images and the idea of empty. "Cruel" is black and frozen and the sting of sizzling whips. "Slaughter" is red and the sucking sound of knives pulled out of beef dripping blood onto a concrete floor.

I remember the first poem I ever felt. I had read poems before and understood them, but never felt them. I was six or seven and it was about a lonely, rainy street and a gray cat in a window with a concrete windowsill. The words affected me so strongly that for an instant I tasted the rain on my tongue and saw the cat and heard its meow above the swish of cars. I actually experienced these things and not the black and white abstractions called words. From that point on, everything I read was compared to that poem. I want to feel that way again. When opening the covers of literary magazines, I grow anxious at the thought of insect words leaping off silk white pages and scratching their way through my eyes. Reading is a constant adventure. I know that doesn't sound original; I don't think it is, but it is desperately true.

For three days she heard the cries. On the first she tried to ignore them. She read an old book and listened to the radio, but they were still there. On the second day, she set about finding where they were coming from. She looked under the couch, between the two windowpanes in the front, behind the refrigerator, and every other place where the cries were not. On the third, she looked in the attic. Wielding a broom because she feared a mouse or bat ...

"I hate library books." She wanted me to look at her, so she said boring things. "I mean, they're all leafed through and dog-eared. Fingered by perhaps hundreds of different people. Murderers, psychopaths, child molesters could have read this."

I pulled my eyes from my plate of shrimp-fried rice and stared at her. "Which group are you in?"

⌖

Everyone's a liar; it's just that writers are honest about it. You know you get stories from writers and poets. Other people make stuff up and don't bother to let you know.

⌖

Chainsaw past exits
and on ramps.
Scathing LCD reminds me
my life pools and hardens
like candle wax
on the table I bought
cheap
at a garage sale.

⌖

The candle wax pooled and hardened on the table in welts and the flame drowned itself as the wick went under. He watched it happen, watched the darkness enter the room. He sat in black for a few minutes, staring into shadows and corners, letting the darkness spread like syrup. Blocks away, a dog barked and pulled him from the shadows. He stood and walked to the lamp, reached under the shade, and clicked the bulb on. The light shined daggers in his eyes and he turned away.

⌖

The old woman pushes the lawn mower up and down the driveway, her pink house coat and dirty white hair flowing behind her. Her combat boots protect her toes from the sharp blades of the mower. Most people drive past her and laugh. Others think it's sad to see an old woman trying to blow the leaves off her driveway. They forget about her and move on.

⌖

The numbers spin in my head and clink together like wind chimes as her monotonous voice drones on and on. She is walking down a dark hallway, and near the end the guillotine stands, its blade glistening as blood from the latest victim of human mind play drips off the edge. As she takes her final steps, she continues to babble mathematical nonsense, unaware of her fate. She kneels down and places her helium head on the blood-stained block, still spewing radicals and tangents. The blade drops, making a clean cut, and her head floats away.

I wish I had a mustache and a beard and was tall and skinny and wore wire glasses and a black and pointed hat and was pale and had black and beady eyes. Then maybe people wouldn't talk to me.

This story—it used to mean something to her. There was something about it that made her carry it around, folded in her pocket, falling apart. Something about one of the characters or the plot—something she could no longer grasp.

Rain poured down on her as she grasped the dipstick in the darkness of the cold night. Grease smeared on her hands and arms as she struggled to pull it out. She couldn't help but think of her father—he had always smelled like this: machine grease and oil. She inhaled deeply and began to let her teardrops mix with raindrops.

He calls himself a crippled Vietnam vet. Now, it's true he is crippled and it's true he's a Vietnam vet, but he's not crippled because he's a Vietnam vet. He and his friends went to a football game, got drunk, and fell out of a tree. My cousin described it best: our family's like peanut brittle; it takes a whole lot of sweetness to hold together all the nuts.

Today on the radio I heard about turkeys. They are so dumb they can't be left in the rain because they turn their heads upward to the sky and swallow rain. Eventually, they drown.

I'm having a hard time with poetry. Images and sylla-bles—it's all too foreign. Fiction is easier because I can use more words. Concise has never been my middle name.

Besides, in grade school poems always rhymed, blatant rhymes like "rose" and "nose." I got used to that; I even liked it. But, like everything else we've learned so far, they teach one thing and then when they think we're old enough to handle it, they tell us the opposite: Washington, father of our country, sainted man. Of course, he was also stupid and a womanizer. Abraham Lincoln wasn't antislavery until after he was elected. And poetry doesn't have to rhyme.

PORTFOLIOS

Portfolios have always been an intrinsic part of an artist's life: that of painters, writers, musicians, anyone involved in the arts. Recently they have also become a staple in English classes throughout the country. In fact, "portfolio" is one of the current buzzwords in edu-cation. This has been both fortunate and unfortunate. It is fortunate in that portfolios are the only reasonable means of assessing the artistic performance of an individual, but it is unfortunate in the ways some persons misuse them.

There are many types of portfolios that may be used for various purposes. However, you may choose to compile one of the following:

1. A showcase portfolio that features the best of your work.

2. A working portfolio that includes many pieces of writing in var-ious stages of revision.

If you become serious about writing, you will no doubt eventual-ly need both kinds. The showcase portfolio is useful when you need to submit work to contests or for entry into workshops, or even for a grade. The working portfolio is your writing lifeline; it holds many pieces in many stages of development. Since writing often needs to "cool" for a period of time between revisions, you may hold onto some pieces for months or even years. You may save a piece that didn't work because there are one or two ideas in it that you wish to return to later. Some pieces may even reside in your portfolio for months before you reheat them. The working portfolio is informal and personal, and you retain sole ownership. You may put into it whatever you wish, and you may discard whatever you wish (although writers seem reluctant to part with paper). Look at your working portfolio as a well that never runs dry.

A LIST OF WRITERS FOR WRITERS

"Only after the writer lets literature shape her can she perhaps shape literature."

Annie Dillard

Reading the classics is an essential part of any writer's education. Writing is an edifice, with each generation building upon the foundation of all that was written before. Fortunately, most schools do an adequate job of acquainting students with classical literature. For the writer, however, the situation is different. Today's young writers must read the most current fiction and poetry available. This work is not found in school anthologies. The most important writing is printed by small literary presses throughout the country. The small press points current writers in the directions that tomorrow's anthologies will echo. Anyone seriously interested in writing fiction or poetry today must become as familiar as possible with some of the names on the following lists. The following list includes some of today's writers who are shaping tomorrow's literature and the names of anthologies where their work can be found:

Yearly Anthologies

The Pushcart Prize: The Best of the Small Presses, edited by
   Bill Henderson
The Best American Short Stories, edited by Katrina Kenison
The Best American Poetry, edited by David Lehman
Poets and Writers Magazine (bimonthly publication with the
   latest in writers and writing)

Short Story Writers

Alice Adams
Margaret Atwood
Rick Bass
Ann Beattie
Richard Bausch
Raymond Carver
Andre Dubus
Louise Erdrich
Richard Ford
Tess Gallagher
Mavis Gallant
Alice Hoffman
Pam Houston

Denis Johnson
Bobbie Ann Mason
Lorrie Moore
Alice Munro
Joyce Carol Oates
Grace Paley
Francine Prose
Lore Segal
Melanie Rae Thon
Anne Tyler
John Updike
Tobias Wolff
Joy Williams

Poets

Margaret Atwood
Marvin Bell
Robert Bly
Gwendolyn Brooks
Raymond Carver
James Dickey
Rita Dove
Carolyn Forche
Tess Gallagher
James Galvin
Louise Glück
Jori Graham
Linda Gregg
Daniel Halpern
Sam Hamill
Edward Hirsch
Garrett Hongo
Rodney Jones
Dorianne Laux
Li-Young Lee
Denise Levertov

Philip Levine
W. S. Merwin
Sharon Olds
Simon Ortiz
Molly Peacock
Marge Piercy
Katha Pollitt
Adrienne Rich
Sherod Santos
Gary Soto
William Stafford
Frank Stanford
Gerald Stern
Leon Stokesbury
Mark Strand
Lucien Stryk
Mae Swenson
James Tate
James Wright
Diane Wakowski

This list is, of course, incomplete. There are many other fine writers, too numerous to mention, whose work merits study.

CHAPTER 2

CHOOSING THE WOOD:
Where Poems Come From

" It goes almost without saying that good hard wood such as oak, maple, cherry or birch is the best to burn. This must be cut in late winter or early spring so that it has the hot summer sun to dry and cure it. It seems a drying and curing period of at least six months is necessary for this. "

Raymond W. Dyer,
The Old Farmer's Almanac

WHAT POETRY ISN'T

"I see no point in picking up pen and paper unless you are going to consign to that paper the truth."

Gwendolyn Brooks

In defining an abstraction, it is often useful to determine first what it is not. This is especially true of poetry. Since every American school child encounters poetry along the way, misconceptions are more common than enlightenment. It seems that no one ever bothers to explain what poetry actually is. As a result, children read it, recognize it, and even memorize it, but they have no idea why and no sense of its connection to their own lives. Some of the following misconceptions may explain why so few Americans either read or write poetry.

Rhyme

Myth #1: Poems have to rhyme:

> Rhyme and meter are devices
> Though neither element suffices
> To carry out intents poetic
> without a consequent emetic.

If asked for a definition of poetry, most people would respond, "lines that rhyme." While this may have been true in the past, free verse accounts for most of the poems written since 1920. In fact, "free" means that the poem is free from formal constraints, especially rhyme. While some poets today choose to work with rhyme at least some of the time, they understand that *rhyme is not an end in itself;* rhyme is a means to discovery. In other words, the poet's goal is not to create long strings of end rhymes, but to use rhyme to push the imagination into new directions that might otherwise not have been explored. Instead of allowing rhyme to dictate meaning, poets use the limitations of rhyme to search for words—the right words—that they would not have considered under other circumstances. Poems written with only the notion that the lines should rhyme quickly turn into doggerel:

> Oh, woe is me, my girlfriend's gone,
> We said good-bye upon the lawn.
> How can I live without her voice?
> But, woe is me, I have no choice!

Free Form

Myth #2: Free verse is simply chopped-up sentences strung along a page. My friend Mort Castle, who coordinates workshops for students and serves as a writing consultant for school districts, says it best:

> Just because
> you shape
> it like a poem
> doesn't mean
> it
> is a
> p
> o
> e
> m

Lost in the Universe

Myth #3: Poetry is whatever you want it to be:

> Where am I going?
> What does life mean?
> Why does no one listen?
> Why does no one care?
> Why is life so painful?
> Why am I so lonely?
> Where can I find love?
> How long must I wait?

The questions may be sincere, but that's all they are: questions, not poetry. There are no images here, no figures of speech, no insight or implication, no interesting use of language—in short, none of the devices of poetry, none of the art.

Yes, Poems Must Be About Something

Myth #4: Poetry is abstract; it means whatever the reader wants it to mean:

> apathy
> fear
> shame

What do these words mean to you?

That question is unfair on every level. Poetry isn't a Rorschach test. It isn't abstract. It isn't vague. It isn't random words on a page. Poetry is as exact and concrete as sculpture, and the poet chooses words just as carefully as the sculptor chooses chisels.

About that *Single Tear*

Myth #5: Poems are usually depressing. Poignant clichés make poems tragic:

A Single Tear

Under the pale moon
a pale maiden
wrapped in diaphanous black
mourned her lost love

In her slender fingers
white as alabaster
she held a wilting rose
red as her blood

Her red red blood ran
along her white white wrists
and mixed with the red
of the rose

Under the pale moon
her face froze to wax
her blood froze to rubies
and, dying, she wept
a single tear

Clichés do not a poem make. In fact, it is precisely because clichés are instantly recognizable by the reader that they are dishonest. The writer has not said what was really meant but has simply borrowed the first easy phrase that came to mind. Even worse, some clichés are noth-

--- A **cliché** is an overused figure of speech. Examples: free as a bird, dark as death, pale moon, raven-haired. Ideas and symbols can also become clichéd. Examples: death wearing a dark hood, a red rose with a thorn symbolizing the pain of love, innocent children with wide eyes looking out at the wicked world.

ing more than cheap tricks, such as the cloying notion of "a single tear." Have you actually seen anyone shed "a single tear"? My students derisively call this sort of clichéd love poem a "rose poem," reflecting the most commonly abused cliché of all.

Poems Don't Teach Lessons

Myth #6: Poems are intended to teach important truths:

Lesson

When I was just a little sprout
I liked to yell and scream and shout
and run around the house with glee
to make my parents follow me.

But now I'm older, nearly grown
and as I've lived the years have shown
the selfless joy that comes with love
and prayers sent to Him above.

With all due apologies to Dear Abby and Ann Landers, poems do not teach lessons. We have sermons, lectures, speeches, essays, abstracts, and informative articles to do that job. Poetry is art, and the role of art is to reflect life, not to teach lessons. Case in point: what lesson do you learn from viewing the Mona Lisa?

☼ FIRESTARTERS

1. On the left side of your paper, list five clichéd expressions; then on the right, create fresh figures of speech to replace them. You may wish to record some of these ideas in your journal to use in future poems. Below are some examples to get you started.

stars like diamonds	hard as nails
sunny disposition	dry as the desert
cuts like a knife	stiff as cardboard
soft as velvet	blanket of snow
sweet as honey	cloak of night

2. Often the idea behind a poem is genuine, but the poet finds he or she has fallen victim to clichés. When this happens, the poet searches for new ways to express the ideas. Try your hand at this type of revision by rereading "A Single Tear" on page 16 and listing all of the clichéd figures of speech and ideas. Choose five clichés and suggest original phrases or ideas to replace them.

3. Reread "Yes, Poems Must Be *About* Something" on pages 15–16. In your journal, list the words *apathy, fear,* and *shame.* After each word write at least five **concrete** details that *show* each abstract feeling. Example: apathy: blank eyes, sagging shoulders, monotone voice, dragging feet, dry cough.   ❧

WHERE DO POEMS COME FROM?

> *"I invited him to Italy this past summer, but he didn't notice anything, anything. It was as if nothing he saw, heard, tasted, smelled, felt, was in any way different from anything he'd seen, heard, tasted, smelled, felt, here in Tulsa. He was unaware, totally and blankly unaware. I couldn't bear it. I can't bear unawareness. I can't. It takes so little, so little, to see . . ."*
>
> *Germaine Greer*

Like wood fuels fire, your life fuels your poems. Your best ideas will come from the world around you, your own personal world. Any subject is suitable for a poem, as long as it is true to your own emotions and experience. However, poets must take nothing for granted; they must look at the world intending to discover the small truths that make poems. Behind every answer, they must see a question; behind every light, they must see a shadow. Unlike greeting cards, which seek to simplify our world and our feelings, poets see the complexities that give richness to our lives. No easy, general observations here; different woods make different fires, and they all burn with differing colors and intensities.

Poets see possibilities where most people see nothing. They feel more deeply and search for insights. The sudden collision of ideas— the twoness of things—is usually the seed of the poem, but the idea

---

--- **Concrete** details are tangible through the five senses: sight, sound, touch, taste, smell.

must be expressed through **imagery**. Poets may begin with abstract ideas, but those ideas must be made concrete through appeals to the five senses, in other words, imagery. The following pages will help you to find ideas for poems in your own life, then suggest some approaches that could work for you. Most of the examples in this book were written by high school students who have learned to open their minds and emotions to poetry.

Michelle Khazai was doing physics homework when she saw how one thing is like another. She toiled at physics with the same agony an infant must feel when it draws its first breath. Physics came hard because she felt the incompleteness of science in explaining the wholeness of life. Intuition told her that life is more than the composite of atoms or the product of theorems:

Laws of Physics

I toil at Physics like a newborn's breath.
The awful collision of atom and atom,
whirring pieces of matter spinning into an anti-universe,
the black void of nothing,
the dip of my hand scooping the canyon's edge.
But theorems can't explain the spotted deer
frozen by my headlights
or the blood flowing creeks and flooding
the abstract design of broken glass
smeared on the highway.
The atoms felt nothing.

A chance encounter at our local bus station gave Brenda Gregoline one of her first poems. Recently discharged patients from the local mental hospital had been medicated sufficiently to warrant their release, but many were still delusional and roamed the streets in constant fear. In her poem, Brenda expresses both her inadequacy and her compassion through strong imagery:

At the elgin bus station

he grabs my coat sleeve,
frenzied eyes smothering mine
with their fire.

- - - **Imagery** is an appeal to any of the five senses.

"the world will end in seven days,"
he slurs, saliva oozing
from his mouth. i tear up my poem
and offer him the pieces.
walking home, i feel the sky crumble.

A few weeks after her experience at the bus station, a friend told Brenda about the time he walked through a sliding glass door. Through wonderfully concrete imagery, Brenda shows how his life has been altered. His accident affected him so deeply that he can no longer trust a door:

Appearances

He told me the story
of how he walked through a sliding glass door.
It looked open, he said.
I think of the betrayal,
his freedom snatched away
and twenty stitches besides.
He remembered the surprise, the noise, the rain
of silver sparkles showering down.
For days he combed glass out of his hair.
Now he wears caution like a too-large hat;
mistrustful of the open door,
he peers around dangerous corners
and knocks before entering.

Eric Johnson had just had an argument with his girlfriend. Even after they thought they settled the problem, something was still wrong. Vivid imagery takes this account beyond the usual teenage love poem. He uses the contrasts of hot and cold to *show* his point. Eric also displays his admiration for "Against Illuminations," a poem by Archibald MacLeish, where two lovers are warned that physical closeness is deceptive; no matter how close the lovers try to be, they are still apart. Had he not read MacLeish, Eric might never have written this poem:

Closed

Last night I locked you out
To keep company with the heartless December air.
I apologized, of course,
With your favorite tea and the warmth
Of our room;

And though the fire has embraced us
With warm arms
And the carpet has absorbed
the long-melted snow from your Nikes,

Still you shiver.
We sit apart, your staring eyes are
Somewhere else;

My attention strays to the door—
Still waiting for you to knock.

Stacey Wiggall was driving to the mall when she saw the twisted wreckage of an accident on the road ahead. The police and tow service were all involved in clearing the intersection. Forgotten, a distance back from the road, lay the canvas-covered remains of a human life. Farther up the road, Stacey saw the unrecognizable body of a small animal left on the highway. She captured the twoness of things in an intense poem chosen for an Illinois Poet Laureate Award by Gwendolyn Brooks:

Roadkill

This autumn sun falls
crisp on the field
tarnishing the leaves
that swirl against my shield of glass
amid the contented color
lies a cold white sheet
covering a shape
I wish was unfamiliar
no broken glass, no puddle of red
no history
only this conclusion
further down there's a rabbit,
maybe a raccoon
belly split open
as this autumn sun shines
the insides
like winter jewels

Stacey's next poem proves that poetry is more than flowers, love, and moonlight. Her subject is a subtle form of child abuse. Stacey had just finished reading a novel where a woman took perverse pleasure from scratching her infant son with a diaper pin:

Scratch

She never read *The National Enquirer*
because she wasn't one of them
those filthy crows
all talons and shrieks.
Her fingers never curled around a knife,
only a safety pin.
No cigarette burns
broken arms
or black eyes,
just a simple dotted line.
One drop of blood would let her sleep.
Afterwards, she kissed his wounds
shuddering to swallow her confession,
her secret.
Delicious.

Erica Knuth's grandmother is Old World Italian. Countless Saturdays in her grandmother's kitchen resulted in this poem. The concrete details and intense concentration on the five senses put the reader right into the kitchen:

Italy

A bit of Italy
flows through the speakers
as Pavarotti's voice
stretches thin across the ocean.
In the kitchen,
red sauce bubbles and spurts
as she stirs the clam sauce
and nurses the linguine.
Pausing to lift her eyes
from the stove to the enshrined Madonna,
she crosses herself with arthritic fingers
curled permanently to fit cooking utensils.
She bakes pasta
stretching to heaven,
lifting her tired bones
to the gates.

Sean McDowell saw a similarity between creativity and food. This
poem came to him after visiting his uncle and aunt, who happens to be

a painter. He realized that both art and food appeal to the senses and captured their essence in words:

What No Restaurant Can Offer

That night was something you
could taste without getting yelled at,
like Godiva chocolates in a jar
or pumpkin pie on the windowsill.
I listened to Lars at the keyboard,
a man possessed with talent
he didn't know he had.
From the past he picked melodies
like grapes and served them
cool in a bowl;
and I painted to the music,
spreading pure color fresh from the tube
like peanut butter across the canvas.
In the next room where the walls
held a buffet of her paintings,
my aunt, the real artist,
slept, bored with our creativity.

Kristen Chambers used the image of a porcelain statue to show a girl about to break. All of the details pertaining to the statue apply to the girl as well and make the reader shiver at "the hairline crack":

Snow White

So fragile
white china sculpted ever so finely
placed in the curio cabinet
among the crystal

Beneath the painted smile
trapped
in the ever so perfect porcelain figure
no one noticed
the hairline crack

Did you notice that none of these poems *tells* the reader what to think? A good poem *shows* its theme through imagery. Poetry is never didactic; that is, it is never written to teach a lesson. Poetry recreates the experience and the feeling so vividly that readers are drawn into the poem to relive the moment of insight with the poet. If the poet has done his or her job, readers draw their own conclusions because they share the experience.

☼ FIRESTARTERS

1. Choose two of the student-written poems above that speak strongly to you. On a piece of paper jot down *why* you react to each poem: which images and words pull you into the experience? Does the poem connect itself to feelings or events in your own life? What senses are used by the poet? Finally, select five words that you believe are most crucial to the poem; explain your choices. Work around the circle in your workshop, allowing students and teacher to discuss their choices until all poems have been covered.

2. List three of your own personal experiences that could make a poem, especially those that pull in the twoness of things. Under each heading also list eight to ten concrete details that could bring your experience to life. Be sure your details pertain to both ideas. Record this assignment in your journal. Here's a hint: when you have an idea for a poem but no time to write it, just jot down the general idea and a list of images in your journal. You will be surprised to find how easily you can write the poem whenever you return to it. The images hold the experience. ☼

Found Poems

Poems are literally waiting for you as nearby as today's newspaper or magazine. Through some judicious editing and careful line breaks, these mundane sources can produce some surprising poems. For example, here is a "found poem" I wrote from a newspaper garage sale ad:

Divorce Sale

Wedding dress, size 6,
veil included;
diamond engagement ring;
maternity clothes, size Small;
Suzuki 800 motorcycle;
nearly new jet skis;
children's clothing, toys, furnishings;
walnut bedroom set

with Kingsize waterbed,
excellent condition.
No reasonable offer refused.
Everything must go.

Depending on the kind of poem you want to write, choose lines and ideas from newspapers, magazines, tabloids, textbooks, catalogs, even operating instructions for appliances. Arrange the lines phrase by phrase for maximum impact. It's easy, fun, and teaches you the way a poem moves—from specific to general. It also gives you an opportunity to manipulate more lines faster than almost any other poem you can write.

Just for fun, I picked up a tabloid newspaper from the supermarket and scanned it for potential poems. Here is just one of the many I found: it blithely reflects the current American distaste for old age:

Jet-set Johnny's wife is all wet!

Johnny Carson's young wife
took a surprise shower
in mid-air.
Blonde beauty Alexis was napping
when a torrent of water
spewed from an air vent
and drenched her.

Her screams of shock jolted
Johnny, who shrugged
and changed seats
with his wife.
The sixty-seven year old
talkshow titan was wearing
a pair of jeans that looked older
than he is. A stewardess quipped,
"It wouldn't have mattered
if they got wet!"

Some students recently found even more intriguing poems. For example, our local newspaper carried an account of a gift shop where plastic statues of the Madonna are said to nod their heads. Sean Dempsey cut just the right lines out of a lengthy article and arranged them with the eye of a poet:

Plastic Madonna

The question dogging hundreds of people
who have seen the six
plastic Madonna statues
at the Angel Kisses gift shop
is simple:
Miracle
or illusion?
The statues nod their heads,
and people agree
the owners, the Kaplans,
are playing no tricks.

Parishioners or their spouses
rejoined the church
after years of apathy
because they saw the statues nod.
The Kaplans think
the miracles protest abortion.

Others seem troubled.
"It bothers me greatly,"
said an Elburn woman.
"It seems very occult.
These are statues.
It's a pagan thing giving power to statues."

Vanessa Ruppert gleaned the following heartbreaking poem from a news article:

Another Myth

Five year old Maria
in the backseat,
playing.
A drunk driver, nameless,
splitting vinyl,
severing her spine.
Overcome with guilt,
mother and brother,
protected
by seat belts,
still walk today.

She splashes water
learning to kick,
builds her upper body
lifting weights,
smiles at cameras
which cut off her body
at the waist.

☼ FIRESTARTERS

Scan the evening newspaper and some popular magazines or tabloids for potential poems. Any printed material is possible fodder for a poem. Cut out articles and tape them into your journal. Experiment with some now to practice movement and line breaks; save others for later poems. Some purists contend that the poet should not delete words or omit ideas in a found poem. For this exercise, feel free to cut and tighten wherever you can. Be relentless. Keep only those words that serve your purpose. An artist takes the raw materials available and hones them into art. Think of your magazine article or advertisement or newspaper column as if it were a slab of marble waiting for a sculptor.   ☼

Poems from Conversations

Poems can also be found in other people's conversations. Illinois State Poet John Knoepfle finds poems in conversations he overhears in his home town, a small town in midstate Illinois near the Sangamon River. As in poems "found" in printed media, Knoepfle edits lines carefully, paying particular attention to line breaks, but he uses some conversations almost verbatim. Knoepfle just sits patiently and *listens* to the speech of the people around him. Of course, he probably records much more than he uses—which is always a good idea. Then he can capitalize on unexpected insights sparked by overheard dialog or select only the best segments of a conversation to fit the theme of his poem.

Study Knoepfle's "watching a haircut," then try your hand at writing an original poem of a place near you. Look for unexpected irony in "found" conversations or tailor snippets of dialog to suit your subject. In either case, be sure to preserve the authentic speech patterns of the speakers.

Your opportunities for observation are as rich as those of John Knoepfle. Look at your home town from a new perspective—that's what poetry is all about. Then choose a locale for your poem. The possibilities are endless.

watching a haircut

they dont put you down
six feet anymore
just forty-two inches
say thats enough now
why its hardly below frost
well they say you cant heave out
the vaults a ton and a half
and what about the water table
how about we get rain for a month
I ask them that and they say
well one did rise up
on polecat creek near chatham
last year first of march
but they was an admiral in it
so it was all right

The lack of punctuation and capitalization here help to preserve the conversational quality. The informality makes the poem *sound* like a conversation overheard in a barbershop.

✸ FIRESTARTERS

Use your journal to record conversations you overhear in your own life. As a writing exercise or a journal entry, try arranging them in lines of free verse following Knoepfle's approach. Be certain that either your title or the early lines of the poem give a sense of the setting. Here are some places you might choose to search for poems in conversations:

gym class
creative writing class
hair salon
concert of any kind, indoors or outdoors
school bus
coffee shop
school cafeteria
garage sale
health club
shopping mall
basketball game
movie theater

bookstore
trendy clothing store
ethnic restaurant
your own kitchen table
bus or train station
airport

Poem Outlines

> *"If I'm not lost after I've gotten lost, I may have*
> *something to talk about and a new place from which*
> *to say it."*
>
> *Steven Dunn*

Below are clusters of images to help you start some poems. These ideas
can be used for practice, in your journal, or for class assignments on
those days when you can't think of anything to write about. Many poets
begin in just this way. They list images, in no particular order, which
they associate with the abstract ideas in their minds. Some images may
not be used at all, others may be added. The important thing, however,
is that the writer has found a starting point and a route to follow
through the poem. Begin by studying a list of images until connecting
ideas begin to flow. Then write, leaving gaps when the right words don't
come. When you have finished, go back and fill in the gaps.

   The first list of images pertains to the Lost Generation of writers
and artists in Paris after World War I. Decide on a feeling or effect you
wish to achieve, then select images to suit your purpose. Add your own
images and connecting words once you know where the poem is going.
Arrange them so they build to a general closure:

Paris
cobblestone streets
1923
chestnut trees on island
The Cafe de Lilas
hotel where Apollinaire died
horse races
boucherie (butcher shop)
smell of wood smoke
The Left Bank

flower sellers' dye running in gutters
The Latin Quarter
The Lost Generation
fish seller's market
Hemingway
zinc bar with cheap wine
femme de menage (cleaning woman)
patisserie (bakery)
bridges arching over Seine
bateau mouche (sightseeing boat)

This second set of images is connected to Wrigley Field, the home of the Chicago Cubs. In your poem you will need to change some of the details exclusive to Wrigley Field to fit your own ballpark. As in the previous poem, arrange your selection of images to create an effect of your own design:

left-field bleachers	Harry Carey
The '84 Cubs	SRO
ivy-covered walls	thick green turf
"Take Me Out to the	umpires in black suits like
Ballgame"	undertakers
bleacher bums	spilled beer
hot dogs	vendors' shouts
Ryne Sandberg	sudden storm off lake
Sheffield Avenue	fat men in shorts
girls in bikini tops	Little Leaguers
die-hard Cub fans	American Dream

☼ FIRESTARTERS

Now make some lists of your own to keep in your journal for a rainy day. Whenever an idea comes, jot down the images, then finish the poem later. You will find that you can recapture the moment with ease.   ☼

INTUITIVE FREEWRITING

> "Each woman has potential access to Rio Abajo Rio, this river beneath the river. She arrives there through deep meditation, dance, writing, painting, prayermaking, singing, drumming, active imagination, or any activity which requires altered consciousness. A woman arrives in this word-between-worlds through yearning and by seeking something she can see just out of the corner of her eye. She arrives there by deeply creative acts, through intentional solitude, and by practice of any of the arts. And even with these well-crafted practices, much of what occurs in this ineffable world remains forever mysterious to us, for it breaks physical laws and rational laws as we know them."
>
> Clarissa Pinkola Estes, Ph.D.

Poetry comes from the right side of the brain, the seat of imagery and intuition. Poetry relies on both of these qualities. Unfortunately, the American school system appeals almost exclusively to the left brain. As a result, many of us grow up unaccustomed to using our right brains, that is, when we consciously call upon them. Every night, however, our right brains transmit the images we see in dreams and even send us the daydreams that arise spontaneously at all the wrong times. It is apparent, then, that all of us have working right brains; we just need to find ways to get that right brain working when we want original ideas. One sure way to tap the images trapped in the right brain is through intuitive freewriting.

The rules are simple: choose any word as a prompt, then write *very* quickly, word by word or phrase by phrase, for about five minutes. Do not write in sentences; do not use punctuation—they are functions of the left brain. Do not plan what you will write. Work solely through association. Whatever words come to mind are the words you write. Ideally, you will write so quickly that you will not know exactly what you have written until you read it. Any time you find yourself thinking about what to write, you can be sure that the left brain is nudging into the process. Push it aside by concentrating only on the next word that flashes into your mind.

Below is an example written by a student named Lisa Morrison. She had just returned from studying in Paris during her junior year in college, where she had lived in the area Hemingway loved so much early in his career. In fact, he was working on *A Moveable Feast,* a nonfiction book about these memories, when he took his own life in 1961. Lisa was sitting in her college library when a bird flew past the window, and she began writing:

fly fly if I could fly pine trees majestic over the field time slips by bye over the mountains and into the blue light of the tunnel vision quest for the fire-eating bearded lady lady walking legs straight as silk and smooth as popsickles melting in the summer sun song sung sweetly in the park park parking lot of your dreams so fly like a bird south like a bird wearing a cap feathered with your friends like banshees wail in the night of your day at midnight half past three time for bed bugs don't bite they tickle your feet but socks made of wool don't get wet in the winter of your eyes when they shine shine like the sea at sunset on the dock holding you back from fate it'll catch you eating lunch of frog legs and sassafras under the willows on the

island in Paris Hemingway loved but look what happened to
him gone blown away like a leaf by his own hands clap after
the final act

Simply freeing the images is an important exercise in itself, but with
your poet's eye you are likely to find a poem lurking beneath the surface
of this seemingly incoherent writing. Remember, Lisa was writing by
word association, so her right brain produced all those words through
some sort of subliminal ordering. Here is the poem Lisa found in her
intuitive freewriting:

Fate

Fate shines
like the Seine at sunset
only the dock holding you
back
It catches you
eating lunch of frog legs
and sassafras
under the willows
on that island in Paris
that Hemingway loved

But look what happened
to him
gone gone
blown away
like a leaf
by his own hand.

Here's how Anna Gregoline discovered a poem using this method:

lightning breaks across my smile in the mirror of my mind
your reflection wavers I wish I knew how to see you right
how to be myself not to hurt you with my tongue with
thoughts with words with pain in joints in brain settles like
leaves and something as strange as autumn in the spring persists I am tired of weather bored with night and day and
silence and noise and wish I could silence you with words as
I do myself

Silence

Lightning breaks
across my smile
in the mirror
of my mind

your reflection wavers
I wish I knew how
to see you right,
how to be myself
how not to hurt you
with my tongue
with pain in joints
in brain
settling like leaves
and something strange
as autumn in spring
persists.
I am tired
of weather
bored with night
and day and silence and noise
and I wish I could
silence you with words
as I do myself.

Over a period of several weeks Kevin Keene developed a poem from
an intuitive freewriting that pulled together some of the emotions and
events that had been churning in his mind. When he began, he had no
idea where the poem, or even the freewriting, would go. As he worked
through several drafts, the poem began to assert itself. The drafts that
follow will show you some of the major stops along the way:

Wall of pine and granite forgiveness carson natl forest gala hills
rembrandt true lies ambition bluebells and sunflowers wild like
a tiger *Sangre Cristo Spanish* keys secrets lies the truth money
sex sex without love or anything reunion *wanderlust* roads
wind whine lama firchado pintura apre I apre I pray absolutely
no regrets I am not sorry hands fish hatching new mexico and
all that good stuff COS Welsenburg Aspen green Taos speeding

hills and two lone wanderers *caring more about me than him*
me than them me than myself opera weddings projects Gustavo
Mike Nebraska *winter* wondering cow sign deer and smart-ass
remarks pertaining to city boys Chicago Carol lateness B. B.
second time around with care pass Questa center trumpet flowers menudo music Greg and groceries my hands smell of
cilantro pesto Chip hummingbirds and homespun Yukon Jack
pickup trucks luck sustenance fortunance mutual funds luck
stovepipe welding English furniture in Mexico cows bulls hay
Blood of Christ retrescado James' all too cute question mark
everything the life Richard Michelle careful full of ____feelings
no regrets emptying my head good weekend life and death row
houses

    It can grow at you. Sitting in front of a piece of paper at
some ludicrous hour wondering, Can I write? What will it be
about this time?

Kevin's first step was to go over his freewriting and circle the images
and words that interested him. (Those phrases are in italics above.)
Then he went to work on the first draft of a poem, still not knowing
where it would lead. Each of his preliminary drafts is filled with deletions, insertions, and changes. However, for the sake of coherence and
readability, only the final result of each drafting session is included here:

Revision 1

In Chicago
We'd love one row and a brick box
I'd mow the lawn
keep steps swept
fill in the cracks
Mother would love our quiet
a sweet south wind

You don't want plaster walls
try pine and granite
forested like winter wheat rows
Other men
"caring more about me than him"
in Sangre Cristo Spanish about us
more about me than myself.

of our holding hands smelling
of cilantro after dinner
sunflowers wild (unfinished)

Revision 2

In Chicago we live in
neat brick boxes
    We die in them too.

I want to mow the lawn
after dying. Policy allows it.
Keep the steps swept
fill in the cracks
Your mother will love you
more like
a sweet south wind
I want my walls out of
plaster
try pine and granite
winter wheat row houses
in the fields fallow
hay stacked
by men whispering
Sangre de Cristo Spanish
you overhear
"caring more about me than him"   —me than myself
while you both hold hands
that smell of cilantro after dinner
and talk of Taos, making love in
Aspen leaves, bluebells,
sunflowers, merry-go-round
not quite lying
but I can't read your mind (unfinished)

—Being away from you
now makes this harder.

Revision 3

In Chicago
we'd live in a brick box
as one. Of many.

I'd mow the lawn,
keep the steps swept,
fill in my cracks.
Mother would love our quiet—
a sweet south wind.

You don't want plaster walls.
Try pine and granite.
Forested like winter wheat rows.

Sangre de Cristo Spanish
winds whisper our holding
hands smelling of cilantro or wild
flowers
fending for ourselves

All told,
being away from you now
makes this harder. Not
"caring more about me than you"
more about me than myself.

Revision 4

In Chicago,
we'd live in a brick box
as one. Of many.

I'd mow the lawn,
keep the steps swept.
Fill in my cracks.
Mother would love our quiet—
a sweet south wind.

You don't want plaster walls
try pine and granite.
Forested like winter wheat rows.

Sangre de Cristo Spanish
winds hear our holding hands
smelling of cilantro
of wild flowers
of fending for ourselves.

Being away from you now makes this harder.
Not, "caring more about me than you,"
more about me than myself.

Revision 5

I Meant to Say . . .

In Chicago,
we'd live in a brick box
as one. Of many.

I'd mow the lawn.
keep the steps swept,
fill in the cracks.
Mother would love our quiet—
a sweet south wind.

You don't want plaster walls
try pine and granite.
Forested like winter wheat rows.

Sangre de Cristo Spanish
winds whisper of our holding hands
smelling of cilantro
of wildflowers
of fending for ourselves.

Being away now makes this harder.
Not, "caring more about me than you,"
more about me than my true self.

☼ FIRESTARTERS

Use your journal to record several intuitive freewritings. Most students find that five minutes is the limit for sustaining the rapid pace. In pieces that interest you, arrange the images in lines of free verse. Break lines at points to create interest, double meanings, lead-ins for the next line. You may find that your intuitive freewriting seems to break up into loosely related segments. That's fine. In crafting your poem, work only with the images that fit together. At this point you may not wish to consider punctuation since your freewriting itself lacked punctuation. That's fine too. First come the images, then come the refinements.   ☼

A CASE HISTORY OF A POEM

"... believing the thing into existence, saying as you
go more than you even hoped you were going to be
able to say, and coming with surprise to an end that
you foreknew only with some sort of emotion ..."

Robert Frost

At a Chicago reading by William Stafford, a man in the audience asked, "Mr. Stafford, what does it take to make a good poem?" "Thirty minutes," the poet said.

Stafford's point is that it is not necessary to know exactly what you want to write until you actually begin the process. Occasionally a poet writes line by line the first time through a poem and has a clear destination in mind. More often, however, the poet begins with images. Since poems originate in the right brain, the seat of all creative activity, and the *right brain thinks in images,* most poets begin by listing images, usually randomly, allowing the poem to develop itself. A basic definition of art is making order out of disorder; your intuition will soon begin putting the images into an order that does, indeed, lead somewhere. You simply need to concentrate intently and trust the muse, for you likely will not know where the poem is going until it gets there!

I began "Road" with only the intention to write a poem and the vague idea of a relationship being as tricky as a difficult road. Through imagery, I wanted to show how some people find the challenge thrilling and others find it threatening. I brainstormed on paper all of the *concrete* ways a road can be both intimidating and exciting:

hairpin curves
hills
mountains
cliffs
deserts
warning signs
blind curves
deserts
valleys
river bluffs
pine trees
river
flooding
danger sign

Then I added details of what I might see, smell, hear, and so on along this road (for example, cactus, white pines, and the like). Soon an order presented itself. The images worked themselves into a coherent order, and the poem appeared, requiring only minor editing:

Road

I am no road for you,
all curves and caution
signs, hills and low spots
prone to flooding.
This road rises to the mountains,
with wild hairpin turns
and peaks
that leave you breathless;
but in between
stone-sheer cliffs and deserts
where no green thing grows
except the cactus.
This road winds along the river,
through gentle bluffs
and groves of white pine,
but you only see the sign,
"Dangerous when wet."
I am no road for you,
with my blind turns
and spiral ascents,
when what you want is good
insurance
and an easy straight.

Sunni Schulz decided to write a poem about a painting, *Cebolla Church,* by Georgia O'Keeffe. The evolution of her poem follows verbatim from the drafts she saved for me to use in this lesson.

Sunni began by listing images:

Notes—Cebolla Church

paper church
plastic pop-art window
jagged roof
metal smokestack
wooden cross
unfolding, a birthday card
pop-up book
construction paper

feather
perfectly sunny day
what if it would rain?
tissue grass
cotton clouds
card folding in on itself
pole holding it up

Her first draft emerged when she added connecting words to the images, and a sense of purpose began to assert itself:

What if it would rain

on the yellow paper church
heavy drops squeezing
from cotton clouds spreading
over the gray roof
sliding off ~~over~~ the warped edges
onto shredded tissue grass
water flooding ~~the~~ cardboard pews
inside, people ~~run streaming through~~ stream
through plastic doors
their cries ~~vibrate~~ shake the walls
pulling free from kindergarten paste,
elmer's glue and a rusting metal
support, ~~a~~ the wooden bell tower
and the ~~painted~~ white matchstick cross
glint in the painted sun
as the church folds in on itself
~~into the crease in the center of the page~~
~~creased into the center of the page~~
creased into the page
as mommy closes the book

Before you continue, look over Sunni's editing in this first draft and consider her reasons for the changes she made.

Three drafts down the line, after sharing her work with other students in the class, Sunni showed me draft four:

storybook church

(what if it would rain)   *stronger*
on the yellow paper church

heavy drops squeeze   // <u>good</u> images!
from cotton clouds, spread<u>ing</u>
over the gray roof
sliding off warped edges
onto tissue grass.
Water floods cardboard pews   *Maybe show that it's melting?*

inside, two dimensional people
strain through plastic doors
their cries shake the walls
pulling free from kindergarten paste,
elmer's glue and slick pages
the <u>glass</u> bell tower   *?*
and white matchstick cross glint
<u>through rain in the painted sun</u>   *? show*
the church folds in on itself
as mommy closes the book

I have duplicated my marks on drafts four and five:

storybook church

i watch rain pelt
the yellow paper church.   *Try dividing into tercets.*
<u>heavy drops squeeze</u>
from cotton clouds, spreading
over the gray roof,
<u>sliding off warped edges</u>
onto tissue grass.   *Good job sharpening*
water floods cardboard pews   *word choices.*
<u>inside, two dimensional people</u>
stream through plastic doors
their cries shake the walls
<u>pulling free from kindergarten paste,</u>
elmer's glue and slick pages.
the matchstick bell tower
and white <u>toothpick cross glint</u>
through rain, unwarmed by the painted sun.
the church folds in on itself
as mommy closes the book.

Because Sunni had chosen to write about a solitary church devoid of people, not much is going on in the poem. The human element is introduced only secondhand by the framework of a mother reading to her child. Sunni risked throwing too much description at her reader in one overwhelming avalanche of images. I suggested that she use interlocking tercets to break up the images. With very little work, Sunni was able present each image as a gem, one at a time, while still connecting them to the same central fabric of the poem.

Voilà! The final product:

storybook church

i watch rain pelt
the yellow paper church
heavy drops squeeze

from cotton clouds, spreading
over the gray roof,
sliding off warped edges

onto tissue grass
water floods cardboard pews
inside, two dimensional people

stream through plastic doors
their cries shake the walls
pulling free from kindergarten paste,

elmer's glue and slick pages
the matchstick bell tower
and white toothpick cross glint

through rain, unwarmed by the painted sun
the church folds in on itself
as mommy closes the book.

☀ FIRESTARTERS

Test Stafford's belief that all you need to begin a poem is a desire to write. Leaf through your journal, looking at previous entries for ideas that can be developed. You need to start with an emotion, then convert it into concrete images. You may find it helpful to begin as I did in "Road," by brainstorming images. Allow your imagination to arrange the images into an associational order. Trust yourself: the linking words and the closure will develop on their own—perhaps not immediately, but over time, as Sunni discovered. Remember, art is a process. File the early drafts of your poem to be revised in lessons to follow.   ☀

CHAPTER 3

PLACING THE LOGS FOR THE FIRE:
The Formalist Tradition

❝ Now place a large log, called the back log, about eight or ten inches in diameter, against the brick back of the fireplace with a little smaller log balanced on top of it. Then place a log about four or six inches in the front of the fireplace just rear of the andirons. This we call the fore log.

❝ Now one proceeds with paper and kindling to build the fire in between the back and fore log gradually building it up to four and six inch logs. **❞**

Raymond W. Dyer,
The Old Farmer's Almanac

A friend who teaches in The University of Iowa Poetry Workshop recently said, "The longer I teach, the more I realize that students need to learn form before free verse." I have long held the same conviction. Why? As a basic explanation, we might say that we need to learn the rules thoroughly before we can break them. As a more sophisticated explanation, we can talk about learning the many elements of poetry and how to use restrictions to our advantage. Without a background in formal poetry, the poet might never discover some of the very tools that will work best in a particular poem. It is the paradox of poetry that restriction creates freedom.

Although free verse is by far the most prominent choice of poets, many fine poets today still work at least some of the time within the formal tradition. Some feel that it keeps them sharply attuned to the many choices within the genre; others believe that formalism propels them into discoveries they would otherwise not make. Still others find that adaptations from the formal tradition give a pleasing form and sound to free verse.

With these truths in mind, the next few lessons will give new poets a background in poetic restrictions that they will actually find liberating—that is, those that allow them to create real art rather than stream-of-consciousness ramblings. Short forms teach economy, sound, and word choice; haiku promotes imagery and intuition; couplets, quatrains, and tercets provide the building blocks of longer forms and introduce new subtleties of rhyme and meter. Sonnets, pantoums, and prose poems provide varied opportunities for form. Some poets will choose to continue honing the formalist tradition; others will move on to free verse, using to full advantage all the arts that traditional poetry can teach us.

CINQUAIN

No more
Your soft endearments
Or warmly measured words
Shall illuminate an empty page
For me.

In elementary school you may have written poems that were word lists arranged in five lines. However, contrary to what many think, the cinquain is more than a poem based on syllable count and composed in five lines, and it is more than a list of adjectives modifying two opposite nouns. It is a delicate verse form capable of carrying a simple but powerful insight. The steadily building structure leads to an abrupt closure that guarantees impact; you just need to word the poem carefully enough to maximize the potential of this form. Forget the cinquains you may have written in childhood; this is a precise poetic form requiring adult subtlety. But here is an insider's secret: if you follow the steps below, you will write mature cinquains the first time around. I guarantee it. Your certain success, along with the attention to sound, content, and precision, make this a perfect place for you to begin your venture into poetry. You will produce poems that please you while you learn important lessons about the language of poetry.

The cinquain form is composed of five lines with the following syllable counts:

> two syllables in the first line
> four syllables in the second line
> six syllables in the third line
> eight syllables in the fourth line
> two syllables in the fifth line

You may bring the lines up to the left-hand margin or spread them out like a Christmas tree. If justified, you may deviate slightly in the syllable counts. Never allow form to dictate content.

However, neither should you settle for the first words that come to mind. The restrictions of the form will actually spur you into thinking of words and sequences of words that would not occur to you otherwise. This form is a concrete introduction into the poet's understanding that formal restrictions are actually springboards that plunge us into ideas and word choices that would never have occurred to us without them. Rather than confining us into straitjackets, they liberate us into new freedom of imagination.

☼ FIRESTARTERS

1. Using all five of your senses, in a list or a piece of freewriting, put down all the concrete details you associate with either a particular place or a particular person.

2. In a list or a piece of freewriting, put down all the abstract feelings you have about either: (1) a fear from your childhood or the present; (2) restriction/freedom in your own life or that of another person; or (3) a subject of your own choosing (an abstraction). Now find a concrete object or set of objects that you associate with the feelings in your abstraction.

3. Select one of the writings above. Set up a comparison between (1) your person/place or abstraction and (2) a concrete object. For example: fear = birds or name = perfume. List many similarities; choose those with the greatest interest or potential.

4. Write your cinquain using the five-line form and the syllable counts described previously.   ☼

Here are some cinquains written by students new to poetry:

Winter Trees

Gnarled
wizard fingers,
glowing in the moon, reach
out to the world enchanted
with snow.
Kathleen Roll

Eggshell

Fingertips
bleed urges,
the membrane between us gone
you've spoiled in my freedom
drip sour
Sean Dempsey

Note how both Kathleen and Sean choose words that work together: fingers reach; eggshell, membrane, spoiled, sour. This unity of metaphor maintains the poem on two levels, the literal and the symbolic, and gives art to the poem.

As in the previous cinquains, Brian uses an extended metaphor. However, he adds another nice touch by using words that speak to each other (that is, words that are pairs of opposites, such as *hot/cold, light/dark, dry/wet, bitter/sweet,* or the affirmative and negative of the same root, such as *agreeable/disagreeable, equal/unequal*):

Her Scent

Her scent
once stung my nose
but now she's gone and I
long for the bitter taste of her
sweet perfume.
Brian Mulliken

☼ FIRESTARTERS

1. Write three cinquains, each extending a metaphor and using words that work together.

2. Write two cinquains using words that speak to each other. Their echoes will add unity to your poems. To get started, make a list of ten sets of words that speak to each other; then allow your imagination to roam. How can these images apply to your own life experience? The answers will come in poems that work on two levels.   ☼

HAIKU

The haiku is an ancient Japanese form based on comparison and syllable count. It requires *intuition* in seeing how one thing is like another. Most often, the haiku is drawn from free association while contemplating nature, always a source of revelation. Occasionally, westerners have expanded nature to include human nature. In either case, the poem forms itself through *images* drawn from the right brain; left brain logic will shoot the wings from your insight and drop it onto the page, unoriginal and dead.

Traditionally, the haiku consists of two images: the first a closely described object in nature, the second a related image that delivers an intuitive insight. The two images must complement one another, each drawing dimension and clarity from the other. Caution: don't try to explain too precisely how the haiku works or "what it means." It means what it is; that's all, and that's enough. Finally, it is important to understand that images and intuition make the poem, not syllable count. It is entirely permissible when writing haiku in English to modify the lines to fit the subject and the image. However, traditional haiku has begun with one line of five syllables followed by a line of seven syllables and then a final line of five syllables for a total of seventeen syllables.

Basho (1644–1738), one of the most venerated haiku masters, saw a likeness between temple bells and flowers. The analogy is intuitive rather than logical, yet startling in its accuracy:

The temple bell stops—
but the sound keeps coming
out of the flowers.

Susan Carbajal draws an imaginative comparison between cymbals and daisies:

Cymbals crash;
daisies with decayed yellow centers
shed petals crisp in death.

Rajul Gandhi creates some remarkable images of his own:

Oh, Tagore!
how I listen all night—
the rain blossoms a cherry.

In poetry even one word speaking
is too much—
Listen, that is enough.

Even the breath of rain
is black—exhaling
dusk in midnight air.

When winter bears
hibernate,
the ground touches snow.

Modern poets often use the haiku as a stanza in longer poems; others write haiku series, where each haiku is separate but related in subject to the others. Joshua Lopez wrote three separate haiku, all reflecting on Indians and hunting. He joined them together in a haiku series that becomes one longer poem:

Hunting Song

Thunder
Like Bison, bodies
Masked in a cloak of fog.

Rain, slow dancing
In lightning's wrath,
Cold as dark kisses.

Wind swift as deer
Joins mothering forest, silenced
By a hunting song.

The line breaks in the first stanza are especially deft. Josh shows that he has learned something about breaking lines for dual meanings. Also, notice how metaphorical his word choices are. He has worked hard to eliminate unnecessary words.

Regardless of the approach you choose to take, haiku is an ideal form for beginning poets who are serious about their art. It concentrates on the essentials of poetry: imagery, intuition, conciseness, sound, and form. Return to the haiku form periodically to keep your senses sharp, your images crisp, and your intuition alive.

☼ FIRESTARTERS

Write three haiku. Perhaps the easiest way to seek inspiration is to place yourself at a window, take a walk outside, or sit for a time on a park bench. Allow your mind to roam freely, making intuitive connections. How is one thing like another? Be very careful, however, not to state explicitly in your haiku what, exactly, the comparison shows. Remember, we are working with intuition. Here are some suggestions for sensory details of nature that might spark a haiku:

the song of a bird	the bark of a dog
the setting sun	the cry of a crow
a drop of rain	a cat hunting at night
a tree stump	squirrels burying acorns
the sound of a locust	the shape of a flower
a worm	the scent of clover
grass blowing in the wind	clouds forming patterns
dried-out wildflowers	crocuses in March snow
a leaf falling to the ground	puddles
wind blowing through willows	the flowing of a river
the shape of bare tree limbs	Queen Anne's lace
mud	ferns
a lagoon	dry wood
a cricket	frogs
the smell of sulfur after lightning	fish jumping

When you have sketched out your idea, go over it carefully. Focus on the images: are they presented as concretely as possible? Now examine the word choices. With only seventeen syllables, you cannot afford to waste even one word. Is each word intrinsic to the poem? Are the words consistent in tone and diction? Finally, read the haiku aloud; does it *sound* like a poem? If not, you may have strung together too many one-syllable words, too many ordinary, unsurprising words, or arranged the words in prosy constructions. Do the sounds of the poem reflect its content? Always remember that words may be moved around within the line or within the poem; you aren't laying cement. Think of your haiku as an illumination rather than a sentence.   ☼

RHYME TIME: *Poetic Devices*

Two of the oldest poetic devices are rhyme and meter, which both focus on sound, since the earliest poems were spoken rather than written. Sound remains one of the most crucial elements in poetry today. Most of us can tell whether a piece of writing being read aloud is prose or poetry. How? Through our innate understanding of how sound operates in a poem.

Most of us grow up thinking that all poems rhyme. Then, during high school, we discover an astonishing fact: most modern poems do not rhyme! We may even sense a certain disdain toward rhyme and other "old-fashioned" sound devices. However, most poets will readily admit that an apprenticeship in formal poetry is necessary even for those who write free verse. Also, perhaps as a reaction to the chaotic social climate, we are moving into a period of renewed interest in formal verse, with many poetry journals today devoted solely to traditional forms.

One of the most valid reasons for studying rhyme is to add new sound devices to free verse poetry. For example, you will begin to find slant rhymes in those free verse poems that sound especially smooth. Modern poets often advise students to consider rhyme as an avenue for discovery. By this they mean that we should not view rhyme as an end in itself. A poem arises out of necessity, an urgency to write about a subject of intense interest. It would be foolish to allow rhyme to control meaning. However, the restrictions of rhyme can push the poet into considering words and ideas that would never have occurred otherwise. This is why poets either work within the restrictions of formal verse or impose their own restrictions under the blanket of free verse.

Rhyme

Rhyme, of course, is an important sound device for the poet. In the old days, when poetry was composed orally, rather than on paper, rhyme was an aid to memory. For that reason, the oldest verse forms employ rhyme and other forms of repetition. Rhyme is repetition of sound, repetition pleasing to the ear. In fact, children enjoy rhyme so much that they often go through a stage of inventing nonsense rhymes. Children's literature abounds with rhyme: witness the success of Dr. Seuss, with his impeccable use of rhyme and meter.

Therefore, rhyme is both pleasant and natural—or it can be, in the right hands. The key is subtlety. The best rhymed poems do not call attention to the rhymes. The last thing a poet wants is for the listener to be distracted into anticipating the next rhyme and ignoring the content of the poem he or she has labored over for so long!

Rhyme comes in many guises, from blatant to discreet:

Masculine rhyme: the rhyme is on the accented syllable. This is the obvious rhyme we are most accustomed to seeing.
Examples: sleet/meet, eager/meager, hollow/follow

Feminine rhyme: the rhyme is followed by an unaccented syllable.
Examples: pupil/fatal, lonely/tawdry

Sight rhyme: words look like they rhyme, but due to changes in spoken English, they no longer sound like they rhyme.
Examples: pain/again, plough/tough, fear/pear

Near rhyme: words don't rhyme, but they sound similar.
Examples: path/grass, fly/behind

Internal rhyme: The rhyming words come inside the lines rather than at the end. This is an excellent unifying device because the rhyme pleases the ear without calling attention to itself.

Slant rhyme: the less obtrusive forms of rhyme, when grouped together.

In discussing rhyme, it is useful to know how to **scan** a poem. When scanning a poem for rhyme, we are concerned only with end rhyme, that is, the rhyming words at the end of lines. All of the forms of rhyme count: masculine, feminine, sight, near, slant. To scan for rhyme, simply read down the right-hand side of the poem and ask yourself whether the last word in each line rhymes with any words at the ends of previous lines. To oversimplify things, let's scan "Twinkle, Twinkle, Little Star":

Twinkle, twinkle, little star, (a)
How I wonder who you are, (a)
Up above the world so high (b)
Like a diamond in the sky. (b)

The rhyme scheme is aabb; that is, line two rhymes with line one and line four rhymes with line three.

Now try your hand at scanning a more sophisticated poem:

That's my last Duchess painted on the wall,	(a)
Looking as if she were alive. I call	(a)
That piece a wonder, now: Fra Pandolf's hands	(b)
Worked busily a day, and there she stands.	(b)
Will't please you sit and look at her? I said	(c)
"Fra Pandolf" by design, for never read	(c)
Strangers like you that pictured countenance,	(d)
The depth and passion of its earnest glance,	(d)
But to myself they turned (since none puts by	(e)
The curtain I have drawn for you, but I)	(e)
And seemed as they would ask me, if they durst,	(f)
How such a glance came there; so, not the first	(f)
Are you to turn and ask thus. Sir, 'twas not	(g)
Her husband's presence only, called that spot	(g)
of joy into the Duchess' cheek; perhaps	(h)
Fra Pandolf chanced to say, "her mantle laps	(h)

These lines from "My Last Duchess" by Robert Browning are written in **couplets**, sets of rhyming lines. Note, however, that this tight rhyme scheme is not at all obvious. If I were to read the lines out loud to you rather than present them scanned on the page, you would very likely not even be aware that the lines rhyme. Browning has maintained a conversational tone throughout by writing lines of ten syllables each that closely resemble the sound of normal English cadence. He has used few **end-stopped lines** where punctuation causes a rest or a stop at the end of the line. Instead, most lines are composed of sentences that carry over into the next line. In this way the end rhymes do not call attention to themselves. Other lines end in slant rhymes such as "countenance" and "glance," which break up any tendency toward a singsong pattern of rhyme.

Among twentieth-century formalist poets, none uses rhyme with greater finesse than Robert Frost. Read his brief poem "The Pasture" and scan it for end rhyme:

The Pasture

I'm going out to clean the pasture spring;
I'll only stop to rake the leaves away
(And wait to watch the water clear, I may):
I shan't be gone long.—You come too.

I'm going out to fetch the little calf
That's standing by the mother. It's so young,

It totters when she licks it with her tongue.
I shan't be gone long.—You come too.

Frost uses the unobtrusive rhyme scheme of abbc deec. The two stanzas are **quatrains**—four rhyming lines of similar meter—with only lines two and three rhyming. This pattern gives an appealing subtlety to the rhyme, unlike the more familiar quatrain pattern of abab, where the end rhyme is obvious. The repetition of the same line to close each quatrain adds unity to the poem and is another sound device. Think about it: rhyme is just another kind of repetition.

As you work your way through couplets, quatrains, and sonnets, try some of the more subtle forms of rhyme. Besides expanding your choices, they may lead you to ideas that surprise even you. Finally, they will give your lines, even free verse lines, a smoothness of sound that you will find missing in the work of those who have not studied sound.

Meter and Verse

Robert Frost used to say that writing poems without meter is like playing tennis without a net. Most poets would agree—even free verse poets—because free verse does have meter, although that meter may be irregular. Once you become sensitive to the rhythms of language, you will intuitively "know" where a syllable more or less is needed in your free verse poem. The only way to attain this skill is to study meter and to read, read, read.

The rhythm or **meter** of poetry is determined by patterns of accented and unaccented syllables. An accented syllable is indicated by a slash and an unaccented syllable is indicated by a crescent. Scan your own name for meter.

Melănĭe   Cămishă   Rĕné   Jeff

Our normal speech is metrical, or we would all speak in a monotone, like Hal the computer in *2001, A Space Odyssey*. To prove this to yourself and to develop an ear for meter, return for a moment to your childhood and scan some nursery rhymes for meter. Read the rhymes out loud, exaggerating the meter, just as you did as a child:

- - - **Meter,** the most important sound device in poetry, is based on patterns of accented and unaccented syllables.

Jack and Jill

Jack and Jill went up the hill
to fetch a pail of water.
Jack fell down and broke his crown,
and Jill came tumbling after.

It is always good practice to read poetry aloud; when studying meter, it is even more important. Listen to your own voice as you chant these rhymes from your childhood. To add emphasis, you may want to tap lightly on your desk as you read: an earnest tap for an accented syllable, a lighter tap for an unaccented syllable. On days when I move from student to student reading various metrical patterns, this is the only way I can keep the poem of the moment in my head. Try this technique with some other familiar nursery rhymes:

Hickory, Dickory, Dock

Hickory, Dickory, Dock.
The mouse ran up the clock.
The clock struck one,
The mouse ran down.
Hickory, Dickory, Dock.

Now scan an old favorite (only the first two lines are done for you; you do the rest):

Humpty Dumpty

Humpty Dumpty sat on a wall.
Humpty Dumpty had a great fall.
All the king's horses
And all the king's men
Couldn't put Humpty together again.

Let's scan a real poem. You will enjoy the lyrical beauty of "Lord Randal," an anonymous ballad from the fifteenth century:

Lord Randal

"Ŏ whére hăe yĕ beén, Lŏrd Rándăl, mў són?
O where hae ye been, my handsome young man?"
"I hae been to the wild wood; mother, make my bed soon,
For I'm weary wi' hunting, and fain wald lie down."

"Where gat ye your dinner, Lord Randal, my son?
Where gat ye your dinner, my handsome young man?"
"I dined wi' my true love; mother, make my bed soon,
For I'm weary wi' hunting, and fain wald lie down."

"What gat ye to your dinner, Lord Randal, my son?
What gat ye to your dinner, my handsome young man?"
"I gat eels boiled in broo; mother, make my bed soon,
For I'm weary wi' hunting, and fain wald lie down."

"What became of your bloodhounds, Lord Randal, my son?
What became of your bloodhounds, my handsome young man?"
"O they swelled and they died; mother, make my bed soon,
For I'm weary wi' hunting, and fain wald lie down."

"O I fear ye are poisoned, Lord Randal, my son!
O I fear ye are poisoned, my handsome young man!"
"O yes! I am poisoned; mother, make my bed soon,
For I'm sick at the heart, and fain wald lie down."

Notice how the whole story is told through implication. Lord Randal's fiancée poisoned him, and now he is going home, heartbroken, to die. The fourth line in each stanza remains the same until the last, where Lord Randal finally reveals that he is not only "weary wi' hunting," but also "sick at the heart." This is the repeat and vary principle, another form of repetition that is used for emphasis.

The most commonly used metrical patterns include the **iamb,** which is the most common meter in the English language. It is composed of one unstressed syllable and one stressed syllable, as in the word *prefer:*

Example: Sómethĭng thĕre ĭs thăt doésn't lŏve ă wáll
Thăt sénds thĕ frózĕn gróund swéll úndĕr ĭt

The meter that most closely follows the natural patterns of spoken English is called **iambic pentameter,** five sets of iambs. In the above example Robert Frost intentionally breaks the metrical pattern with the word *something* to emphasize its importance. That word is the focus of the poem; the successive lines investigate just what it is that does not love a wall. Also, the inverted word order in the first line throws the attention onto "something" by placing it prominently at the beginning of the sentence, rather than the bland construction: "There is something that doesn't love a wall."

Anapest is another popular meter that is composed of two unstressed syllables followed by one stressed syllable:

Example: The Assyrian came down like the wolf on the fold

Other metrical patterns are seen less frequently, but are often used in combination with iambs or anapests.

The **trochi** has one stressed syllable followed by one unstressed syllable, as in the word *fever*.

The **spondi** has two stressed syllables, as in the word *heartache*.

The **dactyl** has one stressed syllable followed by two unstressed syllables, as in the word *eagerly*. The dactyl is used in the original Greek verses of *The Iliad* and *The Odyssey* since it most closely reflects the meter of the Greek language.

The **amphibrach** has one unstressed syllable, one stressed syllable, and another unstressed syllable, as in the word *complaining*.

When the meter is very regular, we call it **strict**; when the meter is less regular, we call it **loose**. Poets often use loose meter to break up a tendency to singsongy lines, especially in closely rhymed verse forms.

Lines of poetry are measured in **feet**. Each metrical set constitutes one poetic foot. The number of feet in each line is indicated by a Greek name. The examples below are based on iambic feet:

monometer: one foot
dimeter: two feet
trimeter: three feet
tetrameter: four feet
pentameter: five feet
hexameter: six feet

The following are common verse forms:

Couplet: two rhyming lines of similar length and meter.
Triplet: three rhyming lines of similar length and meter.
Quatrain: a poem or stanza of four lines, where at least the second and fourth lines rhyme. Quatrains are often used to build longer

poems. Example: ballads written in four iambic feet in both the first and third lines, with three iambic feet in the second and fourth lines. Possible variations include aabb, abab, abba, abcb; or rhyme schemes that interlock the stanzas, such as abab, bcbc.

Blank verse: unrhymed iambic pentameter.

Free verse: unrhymed, irregular in form, although it must have some meter.

Octave: an eight-line verse; usually the first part of a Petrarchan sonnet.

Sestet: a six-line verse; usually the second part of a Petrarchan sonnet.

Tercet: a stanza of three lines, either rhymed or unrhymed. When rhymed it is usually used in an interlocking rhyme scheme for a longer poem.

Sonnet: a fourteen-line iambic pentameter poem. In the Petrarchan version there is a clear break between the octave and the sestet. The octave states a question, doubt, thought, or wish, and the sestet answers or responds to the octave. Octaves rhyme abba abba; the sestets rhyme cdecde, cdcdcd, or cdeedc. The Shakespearean sonnet is less rigid in form. It is written much like three related quatrains closing with a couplet. Usually, the couplet summarizes, answers, or contrasts with the rest of the poem. The rhyme scheme is abab cdcd efef gg. The modern sonnet retains the fourteen line structure but may not be rhymed or strictly metered.

☼ FIRESTARTERS

Use this reference guide as you work your way through assignments. Even if, like most modern poets, your goal is free verse, you will need to incorporate these techniques into your work. Free verse is never so free that it eliminates all formal considerations. You will also find that these basic verse forms can become the building blocks to long poems. Use the models on the following pages to write couplets and quatrains in order to build your way to a sonnet.   ☼

Couplets and Quatrains

Although you may be unlikely to write couplets or quatrains as single poems, you will find them essential in composing longer poems. For example, a Shakespearean sonnet is nothing more than three related quatrains followed by a couplet. Considering the recent interest in formal poetry, you will want to master these essential short forms.

Traditionally, a couplet is a two-line poem using rhyme and meter. Many longer poems are nothing more than a series of rhymed couplets. If the poet is very good, you may not even be aware of the rhyme.

Here, Richard Towry writes a wry couplet:

Rap It Up

Someone put him on the shelf;
Now he's choking on himself.

You may find quatrains easier than couplets; you have twice as much room to say something coherent. The four lines must be metered and rhymed. Some rhyme choices include aabb, abba, abab, abcb.

Again, Rich manages to be clever within severe restrictions:

Yes, Sir William

I'm not so dull, 'tis but my job;
I see you in a shapeless blob
Of dust and damp, of beaut and rue—
By right of pen, a poet true.

Here's a hint for first-time rhymers. If you can't find a rhyme for the line the way it's written, try moving words around within the line. Some words are much easier to rhyme than others. Rich moved "true" to the end of the last line, and the poem works. The unusual word order seems appropriate for the subject of the poem. That, of course, is the key: matching form to content.

☼ FIRESTARTERS

Write two couplets and two quatrains. Use variations of rhyme and meter to suit the subjects of your poems.   ☼

SONNETS

The sonnet is the crown jewel of formal poetry. It is the traditional form for love poems, dating back to Petrarch and Laura in Renaissance Italy. Petrarch saw Laura, a married noblewoman, only once, as they passed while crossing a bridge. It is likely that she hardly noticed him, but her beauty inspired a new art form. Over the years, Petrarch wrote over three hundred sonnets that immortalized Laura. Later, in Elizabethan

England, Shakespeare wrote love sonnets for his "dark lady," a mystery woman with dark hair and complexion. In mid-nineteenth century England, Elizabeth Barrett Browning wrote a sequence of love sonnets to her husband, Robert Browning, who literally rescued her from imprisonment in her father's home. More recently, Chilean poet Pablo Neruda wrote one hundred sonnets of incredible beauty for his love, Matilda Urrutia.

Although love is a frequent subject for the sonnet form, it is by no means the only appropriate subject. The formality of the sonnet seems to invite serious themes, but Shakespeare, among others, shows us that sonnets can be playful, even humorous. Among the sonnets below you will find variety in subject, tone, and form. They vary from the strictly formal to the riskily modern, but all are well written, carefully executed, and finely revised. Choose the form that suits you best: Petrarchan (Italian), Shakespearean, or modern. Then make the sonnet work for you.

The traditional **Petrarchan sonnet** is written in iambic pentameter, divided into an octave (eight lines) and a sestet (six lines) with a strict rhyme scheme: abba abba cdc cdc. (The sestet allows other variations; see page 61.) The octave presents a question or situation, and the sestet answers the question or reflects another view of the situation. In a classical Petrarchan sonnet, from *Sonnets from the Portuguese,* a collection of love poems for her husband, Elizabeth Barrett Browning reflects upon what people mean by "love." She does not want to be loved for physical beauty or an appealing personality trait, or even because of her husband's compassion, for these things can change. She asks, simply, that he love her for love's sake:

If Thou Must Love Me

If thou must love me, let it be for naught
Except for love's sake only. Do not say,
"I love her for her smile—her look—her way
Of speaking gently—for a trick of thought
That falls in well with mine, and certes brought
A sense of pleasant ease on such a day"—
For these things in themselves, Beloved, may
Be changed, or change for thee—and love, so wrought,
May be unwrought so. Neither love me for
Thine own dear pity's wiping my cheeks dry—
A creature might forget to weep, who bore
Thy comfort long, and lose thy love thereby!
But love me for love's sake, that evermore
Thou mayst love on, through love's eternity.

In a modern adaptation, Pablo Neruda maintains the traditional octave and sestet while omitting the rhyme and regular meter:

VII

Come with me, I said, and no one knew
where, or how my pain throbbed,
no carnations or barcaroles for me,
only a wound that love had opened.

I said it again: *Come with me,* as if I were dying,
and no one saw the moon that bled in my mouth
or the blood that rose into the silence
O Love, now we can forget the star that has such thorns!

That is why, when I heard your voice repeat
Come with me, it was as if you had let loose
the grief, the love, the fury of a cork-trapped wine
that geysers flooding from deep in its vault:
in my mouth I felt the taste of fire again,
of blood and carnations, of rock and scald.

Denny Neiman follows the Petrarchan form closely, varying the rhyme scheme only slightly and keeping his lines at ten or, occasionally, eleven syllables. Note the slight shift between the octave and the sestet:

Quickly comes tomorrow, faster the day after

Is tomorrow a day that has yet to come
in order of meter and/or with rhyme,
always extended over a given time
which is skimpy, meager, much like a crumb
in a slice of bread previously eaten,
gone, without trace, but used with good taste?
For some, it is gone, a forgotten waste,
their competitor, a clock fast beaten.
One's life is but a drop in a river
of time most swift that will never cease flow.
Its path follows rocky currents of fate
to pools of calm, but means to be late.
It is then, when it stops, that we will go
to a whole eternal, from a sliver.

Chris Newton modifies the Petrarchan rhyme scheme into his own version of an octave and a sestet. To keep the poem conversational,

Chris is careful not to use exclusively end-stopped lines. By carrying thoughts over to the next line, he avoids singsong iambs. This modern sonnet won honors from both the Columbia Writing Awards and the Illinois Association of Teachers of English:

If I Were a Better Poet, I'd Be Published

If I were a better poet, I'd be published;
throw in similes, impulsive like trash
during storms. I'd use strong verbs like slash,
flesh with scarlet gashes, say the faucet hissed
a man's steamed anger towards the woman
who left him drained of life and crying
alone. It wouldn't be about dying;
love seems obsolete, six feet from the sun.
I'd use images, concrete, like my dad's fingers;
he was a carpenter by trade, and every
day he'd drive nails into me. I see
critics, disgusted. I follow their fingers,
nothing's spoken. They just nod. With his style,
maybe Hallmark, they think, and just smile.

Here's your payoff for all that practice with quatrains and couplets. The **Shakespearean sonnet** is simply three related quatrains followed by a couplet. The rhyme scheme easily divides the poem for the reader: abab cdcd efef gg. The three quatrains present three views of a subject, and the couplet concludes the observation. The poem may be written in a block of fourteen lines or divided into stanzas.

Shakespeare wrote Sonnet 29 to show his appreciation for the support of his patron:

Sonnet 29

When in disgrace with Fortune and men's eyes,
I all alone beweep my outcast state,
And trouble deaf heaven with my bootless cries,
And look upon myself and curse my fate,
Wishing me like to one more rich in hope,
Featur'd like him, like him with friends possess'd,
Desiring this man's art and that man's scope,
With what I most enjoy contented least;
Yet in these thoughts myself almost despising,
Haply I think on thee; and then my state,
Like to the lark at break of day arising

From sullen earth, sings hymns at heaven's gate;
For thy sweet love rememb'red such wealth brings
That then I scorn to change my state with kings.

Draw a line under the fourth, eighth, and twelfth lines; then examine Sonnet 29 like a jeweler examines a diamond: hold it up to the light and turn it slowly. Each quatrain is another facet of the same gem; the couplet is the final assessment. In the three quatrains, Shakespeare feels despair because he lacks the privileges and attributes of other men; then in the couplet he looks to his good fortune at having his patron to support him and celebrates.

Sunni Schulz uses slant rhyme in the classical Shakespearean manner but shortens the lines from the standard ten syllables and avoids using many end-stopped lines. The result is a sonnet that reads smoothly without calling attention to its form:

watercolored

the girl with cherry hair blossoms
out of her flowered hat curling
over narrow shoulders roams
wearing her mother's criticism swirling
around slender ankles like tide
pools rising to cover skinned knees.
the sun melts red from a watercolored sky,
she struggles against the current of the sea.
tears shatter her visions of perfection
salt stings her open wounds
bleeding caution, she adjusts her reflection
in her mother's eyes, no sounds
but the slap of wind which mocks
waves tossed against jagged rocks.

Charles Noback modifies the Shakespearean sonnet by eliminating rhyme, except in the couplet. His lines are not iambic pentameter, but are of similar length and weight. In an interesting twist, he has borrowed the double line breaks and interlocking stanzas of free verse. Each line presents a single image that expands into a second image when read with the succeeding line. In the same way, the stanzas also work both separately and together:

Old South

Leaves crunch as you trudge under a canopy of trees
lining an unused path, once gateway to dreams.
Gothic windows stare, "Are you the master?"

in the fields slaves pick cotton, bolls in fingers
drip sorrowful; blood runs down your arm staining
picked cotton in canvas sacks rustling, "Tired?"

music flits out open doors, the dance begins.
Ladies curtsey in dresses of canary yellow,
Men in confederate uniforms, "Care to dance?

with fire black boy?" Ghost knights draped in white,
a burning cross daggers the earth, casting
flickering darkness. Flames leap onto terrified people

and the house. Only the frame hangs tacked
against silent skies. Footsteps echo your way back.

☀ FIRESTARTERS

You are ready to write your own sonnet—as strictly or as loosely as
your subject and your temperament demand. Either way, you will find
that restrictions actually add power to your work. There's no room to
ramble in a sonnet. Sonnets deliver direct hits.   ☀

PANTOUM

The pantoum is a Malayan poetic form that appeared in the fifteenth
century. It surfaced later in France and England and was popularized in
the United States by John Ashbery in *Some Trees,* published in 1956.

The trick to the pantoum is finding versatile lines that may be
repeated without weariness and used in many contexts. Both the delight
and the bane of the form is the repetition of lines, which is mesmerizing
if used deftly and deadly if used clumsily.

In its western incarnation, the pantoum is of indeterminate length,
but at least three or four stanzas are necessary to set up the pattern of
repetition. The form does allow for variation, especially in the last stanza, where, traditionally, the second and fourth lines repeat those in the
first stanza. Michelle, like many modern poets, chose not to follow this

tradition. Rhyme is optional. However, a word of caution: if rhyme is used, it must be subtle. Monotony could easily result from too heavy-handed a combination of repetition and rhyme.

The basic form follows:

Line 1
Line 2
Line 3
Line 4

Line 5 same as Line 2
Line 6
Line 7 same as Line 4
Line 8

Line 9 same as Line 6
Line 10
Line 11 same as Line 8
Line 12

The pattern continues until the poem is completed. The last stanza may contain second and fourth lines that are the same as the first and third lines of the first stanza. In this way, the poem runs a complete circle, ending where it began.

Michelle Van Ness wrote the following poem when she first began experimenting with pantoum:

Crayon Scratches

This drawing of my brother is incorrect:
his smile much wider than sincere,
eyes heavy without sleep, hands too large
looking awkward resting on his knees.

His smile much wider than sincere,
he giggles high notes on the piano.
Looking awkward, resting on his knees
I sketch his outline beneath the windowsill.

He giggles high notes on the piano
as if he could perform concertos with crickets;
I sketch his outline beneath the windowsill.
Sun warms his hair and shadows wrinkle his shirt.

As if he could perform concertos with crickets,
dust practices flying with breezes while

sun warms his hair and shadows wrinkle his shirt.
Crayon scratching, he eyes its green marks;

Dust practices flying with breezes while
this drawing of my brother is incorrect:
crayon scratching, he eyes its green marks;
eyes heavy, without sleep, hands too large.

Here is one of several pantoums written recently by Aaron Anstett.
He uses the difficult circular pattern of echoing the first and third lines
of the poem in his last stanza:

Then

A moment the pornography of a moment
The *as if,* the likeness, spirited in flesh.
As if loving less made leaving easier.
The one walking away walks in a shared light.

The *as if,* the likeness, spirited in flesh.
Meat of the apple unwound.
The one walking away walks in a shared light.
Darkness its own nation state.

Meat of the apple unwound.
The maples look lovelier drunk.
Darkness its own nation state.
They rose shorn, calling out to be covered.

The maples look lovelier drunk.
A world tilts in the blood.
They rose shorn, calling out to be covered.
Not to be dwelled on, breathing as labor.

A world tilts in the blood.
Under the earth, more earth.
Not to be dwelled on, breathing as labor.
Ablative grace, like a current through water.

Under the earth, more earth.
Catalog called *The Tortures.*
Ablative grace, like a current through water.
Flooded villages slow to burn.

Catalog called *The Tortures.*
String of brief enthusiasms.
Flooded villages slow to burn.
Every face betrays its bearer.

String of brief enthusiasms.
A moment the pornography of a moment.
Every face betrays its bearer.
As if loving less made leaving easier.

☀ FIRESTARTERS

Experiment with the pantoum. You will find that the restrictions of the form will force you to consider words and lines carefully, for sound as well as for meaning. You will need to compose lines that adapt themselves to more than one use. If you use the circular pattern of repeating the first and third lines of the first stanza in the second and fourth lines of the last stanza, the lines must function both as an opening and a closure. ☀

PROSE POEM

Some writers define prose as anything that isn't poetry and poetry as anything that isn't prose. The prose poem fills the shadowy area where the two genres merge. A comparatively recent form, the prose poem does indeed blur the lines between poetry and prose. Perhaps it reflects the growing number of writers who choose to work in both genres. It is written in paragraph form, so it is prose—right? It employs all the devices of a poem, so it is poetry—right? In fact, it is a hybrid, but with more acreage in the poetry camp. Study the examples below. While the form seems to be the familiar sentences of prose, everything else is poetry—imagery, repetition, figures of speech, implication—and the piece *moves* and *sounds* like a poem.

When two former students and I began *Bluff City* in 1990, we wanted to create a forum where risks could be taken, where new ideas were welcome, but where high standards of writing were preserved. As part of our approach, we created a mythical small town, Bluff City, as the setting for our magazine. The name itself was a double entendre: Elgin, our home base, is located on a river bluff, and the whole idea of Bluff City is a fabrication. To portray our unique perspective, we decided to begin each issue with a prose poem introducing a resident of Bluff City. The prose poem seemed to be a natural format since *Bluff City* is "a magazine of poetry and prose." Consider the following example by Luis Hernandez:

If you walk the edge of this town, you figure out quick it ain't no razor, a cracked bowl, maybe. There's places to fall around here, but you're not likely to get hurt. Near dawn, I'm sitting in the fields near the Bluff City I.D.T. station. Not sure what I.D.T. stands for, but it sure knows how to hum. I've wired boards to the fence to break the breeze, and in the blue mornings, just before the humming starts, I count stars in the eyes of rabbits. Sometimes I've counted hundreds inside those dark globes. By noon I'm in the center of Bluff City, arms wide and gathering air. Mikey and Jet have been watching for the past couple weeks, and when I'm close to falling, they close their eyes and pretend to feel the warmth. I start spinning slowly, then release almost everything. Thin red light outlines my bones, and it's all I'm keeping for myself. Mikey and Jet say I should be mayor.

The results were equally good when my students tried the form. They enjoyed working with this new approach.

Wanchay Chanthadouangsy has always been torn between poetry and prose, so the middle ground of the prose poem is ideal for her:

Cut and Dry

It hurts when you cry. You tell me that as we sit on your kitchen floor, you chopping onions and me watching your eyes, dry as the moon. The vapor should have reddened them, should have dropped your tears one by one. But you are the man and I sit waiting with open palms ready to catch anything willing to fall.

Your knife, pounding through onion and board, vibrating into my bare knees that would have collapsed if I were standing. But I know you would have saved me from the fall. Your eyes would have searched for where it hurt but would remain as cold as the blade now catching the sun with each downward motion, glinting the warnings only I know. Your long fingers stretch too close to the blade. I could snatch your hand away, prevent pain to those fingers, but I want to know if you'd scream, if you'd close your eyes and cry out for me to cradle you in my arms, let your pain soak into my hair. And I'd kiss those fingers and those salty tears hinting of onions.

But you are too careful. Your task is finished before mine. The onions are in a bowl. The board and knife are in the sink. You say you'll wash them later, but I know you won't come back. I will wash this knife for you today and every day. I will slice my fingers against the edge. The pain can't last long. I will dare to do what you cannot.

Judith Lloyd responded to the assignment with a prose poem loaded with metaphor:

Strange Cravings

She hates her hair. She despises it more than green olives or week-old meatloaf. She stands at the counter, watching syrup drip down the sides of the waffle like thick blood. He sits at the table, waiting for her to speak. Her voice does not come, so he turns and looks out the window, searching the night sky. There are stars. He tells her. She does not say a word. He pushes his Coke with his thumb and traces a word into the water that trails behind: late. She squeezes the syrup bottle, trying to get more.

Her hair falls in her face. She smacks the bottom of the syrup bottle, trying to get something when they can both see it's empty. She is angry. She says he should have bought more syrup. He tells her there's more in the cabinet above the stove. She doesn't seem to hear him. She stops squeezing the bottle and sets it down. She picks up her plate and turns to the table, he watches her hair drop in front of her eyes. The fork on her plate is covered with syrup. She picks it up, turns it sideways, and pushes it into the waffle, splitting a piece away.

He asks if she is all right. She cuts into her waffle again. He looks back down at the table and draws circles in the water. She asks him if he wants a waffle. He tells her he's not hungry. She shoves the fork into her mouth. She chews and makes a face. She says it's too sweet, turns, and looks out the window. He asks if she can see the stars. She squints and says she can. She tells him that she once tried to learn the constellations from a book, but could never find the right stars. She tells him that she was going to take astronomy in college. She looks back down at the table and stares at her plate. There's no syrup left in the bottle, she says, her eyes watering.

He tells her that she could still go to college. She shakes her head and puts a hand over her face. He pushes his chair back without touching the table. He gets up and walks over to her. He puts his arms around her. She looks at the back door and slides out of his arms. She walks to the door and stares out of the screen. He thinks of hair sweeping her bare shoulders as the wind brushes it back. She presses her fingers to the door until it opens. She steps out of the house and he follows her into the backyard. She stops under the apple tree and looks up at the sky. He stops behind her, smelling her hair. He asks if she can find the north star. She nods and points south. He takes her by the shoulders and turns her, guiding her hand across the stars. She tells him she can see it. She says it's very bright. He sees the diamond in her ear and thinks of the ring on his mother's left hand. She tells him she always wanted to see the big dipper. He helps her find it.

Wind whispers in their ears and knocks blossoms from the apple tree. They sit crosslegged on the grass, then lie down. Grass prickles their necks as they lay side by side, watching stars flicker out, one by one.

☼ FIRESTARTERS

Write your own prose poem, using the examples above as models. You may choose to write in third person like Luis Hernandez in *Bluff City,* in first person like Wanchay in "Cut and Dry," or even try your hand at second person, the journalistic "you." Regardless of the point of view you choose, the manuscript conventions of prose will extend the range of your poetry. ☼

CHAPTER 4

LAYING A BED FOR THE FIRE:
Free Verse

> **"**To build a fire properly, for one of good steady heat with a small blaze and minimum use of wood, the whole fireplace should be covered with a good bed of ashes about one or two inches above the andirons. **"**
>
> Raymond W. Dyer,
> *The Old Farmer's Almanac*

70

Open a book of poetry today, and you are likely to find free verse. The modern temperament seems to resist the traditional forms of the past and demand a more vigorous and personal approach to poetry. However, in poetry as in life, freedom from old restrictions requires the application of new restrictions. **Free verse** simply means that the poem is free of rhyme and regular meter; it does not imply that the poet is free to ignore all poetic constraints. In fact, poets must adhere even more closely to those poetic conventions that remain: imagery, sound, unity, conciseness; they may even find that they must invent new formal restrictions. When the thirteen colonies rebelled against the English monarchy and overthrew the king, they immediately replaced the old government with a new constitution. The poet must do the same. In art, as in government, chaos leads to disaster.

Not surprisingly, the free verse movement gained momentum during the period following World War I. In the early 1920s, Paris was a cauldron of artistic activity that produced sweeping changes in painting, music, poetry, short stories, and novels. Young artists who had been deeply affected by the war felt that art should reflect the changes they saw in themselves and in society. They questioned the old ways, the traditional forms that suddenly seemed out of step with the modern world. Pablo Picasso led the way to abstract art; Ernest Hemingway refined the short story; James Joyce revitalized the novel; Erik Satie experimented in music; and free verse poetry was born through the early efforts of e. e. cummings, T. S. Eliot, and others.

Most of us associate e. e. cummings with popularizing free verse. He experimented with line breaks, capitalization, punctuation, and even invented his own hyphenated words. He abandoned all the rules—or did he? Examine his poem "Sonnet," and, beneath the apparent guise of free verse lines, you will find a traditional Shakespearean sonnet without capitalization. He even uses rhyme, but so subtly that you may not notice it in a first reading:

Sonnet

a wind has blown the rain away and blown
the sky away and all the leaves away,
and the trees stand. I think i too have known
autumn too long

        (and what have you to say,
wind wind wind—did you love somebody
And have you the petal of somewhere in your heart
pinched from dumb summer?

> O crazy daddy
> of death dance cruelly for us and start
> the last leaf whirling in the final brain
>
> of air) Let us as we have seen see
> doom's integration . . . a wind has blown the rain
>
> away and the leaves and the sky and the
> trees stand:
>   the trees stand. The trees
> suddenly wait against the moon's face.

Examine his popular "in Just-," and you will find a peculiar situation: cummings dispensed with ordinary capitalization and devised his own system. Some words are capitalized. Why? The important lesson here is to see that he had good reasons for the rules he abandoned and good reasons for the rules he created. Free verse is not composed according to whim; it is composed according to reason:

in Just-

in Just-
spring   when the world is mud-
luscious the little
lame balloonman

whistles   far   and wee

and eddieandbill come
running from marbles and
piracies and it's
spring

when the world is puddle-wonderful

the queer
old balloonman whistles
far   and   wee
and bettyandisbel come dancing

from hop-scotch and jump-rope and

it's
spring
and
  the

        goat-footed

    balloonMan   whistles
    far
    and
    wee

What "rules" or constraints did cummings set up for himself? How did he decide which words to capitalize? What new words did he create with hyphens? Why wouldn't existing words do? Why does he run together the names of the children? Why does he run ideas together as if they are one long sentence? What classical **allusion** to mythology is at the heart of this most modern of poems?

It is not surprising that the imagist movement grew out of the free verse furor. Without the guidelines of traditional form and conventions, poets realized that other poetic devices must drive the poem. The imagists juxtaposed two concrete images to fuse into a sudden illumination. Even today, following this imagist legacy, most poets insist that imagery is the focus of the poem. They strive for a unity of images to create a tension that builds throughout the poem.

The line break took on new importance with the birth of free verse. Unencumbered by prescribed forms that meted out syllables like dollars, poets found that they needed to rethink the rules. New opportunities arose as they found that line breaks could create dual meanings; each line could work alone, then unfold into an extended meaning when read with the following line. Poets found that lines had to end with a word strong enough to pull the reader into the next line—usually a noun or a verb. Already they were working out new restrictions.

Finally, sound took on new complexity. Without the familiar tool of masculine rhyme, other sound devices were needed. Poets found themselves listening more closely to the sounds that words and letters make, found themselves projecting tone through sound. Word choice became increasingly important; they had to consider the way words sound as well as what words mean. Without careful attention to sound, their poems could read like prose. They grew relentless in cutting away glue words or weak words; they became aware of the necessity of patterning their words, their lines, and their poems. They looked for parallelism, strong repetition, and words that speak to each other. They found that free form is form after all.

Because of its nebulous rules, free verse requires a longer apprenticeship than formal poetry. Your best means of learning is simply to

---

- - - An **allusion** is an indirect reference.

read and analyze successful poems: poems written by famous poets, poems written by obscure poets, poems written by other students. Find poems that work and study them. Find poets you admire and study them. Read collections of work by one poet, glean what you can, then move on to another. Use your journal to record observations; use class time to discuss what you find.

Student-written models provide a good starting point. Since they are written by young poets, they present a level of skill within the reach of other students. Even more important, they prove that young poets can write fine poems and that young poets are right to aspire.

Brenda Gregoline was a recent first-place winner in the Scholastic Writing Awards. The following poem also won top national honors in free form poetry in the Columbia Writing Awards:

Dusk

Night arrives from the ground up
shadows rise out of the grass
shaking dust from their muted limbs
The in-between hour, hushed and expectant
when children halt touch football games
thinking: Something is going to happen
When even the commuters worrying towards home
start to believe in Art and Fate
When bag boys at Jewel, pieces of poetry
flickering in their minds, ignore scattered carts
to watch light fade and darkness wash in
Stars are slowly being born
and all over the city faces turn upwards in hope
everyone making wishes, remembering secrets
everyone believing in his own luck.

Analyze "Dusk," either in class or by yourself. Refer back to the earlier section of this lesson for ideas. Read down the right-hand side of the poem; not a weak word there. Look at the poem without reading it. That's right; just look. Do you notice all those vowels? How do these repeated vowel sounds—assonance—project the mood of the poem? How do some words and some lines slow you down? How well does the pace match the content? On your own paper list your five favorite word choices. Why these five words? Why are Art and Fate capitalized? How is "worrying" used differently here? Describe the pictures you see in your mind as you consider the poem. How do the images work together? What is their common thread?

Brenda's poem that follows is a favorite with most students:

in the hospital waiting room

your dad in intensive care,
you clung to me like a last hope.
My arms were wide and strong as ocean.
I handed you kleenex while you sobbed in my lap,
stroking your hair
and feeling absurdly maternal.
Now your relatives have arrived
and I am the outsider.

They swarm over you, offering comfort and advice.
They invade you like a country.
They hold both your hands
and toss suspicious smiles in my direction—
Who is she?
I am a jealous bird, perched in the far corner of the couch.
I am outdated and useless,
a burnt loaf of bread
a bike with only one wheel.
I have been fired
from the job of loving you.

Write out Brenda's poem on a piece of paper. Circle all the images. Is
the poem covered with circles? Now draw a line under the strong word
choices. Is the poem riddled with lines? Mark a wavy line under surprising images. Lots of wavy lines? Point arrows at **parallel** phrases and
lines. Is the page full of arrows?

End of lesson. You are ready to begin a reading campaign of your
own.

SEEING THE TWONESS OF THINGS

Ask a poet how a poem begins, and he or she is likely to talk about connections, the flash of insight about how *one thing is like another*. This
twoness is the basis of all comparisons, all figures of speech, all symbols,

---

- - - **Parallel** phrases or lines are words, clauses, or sentences of similar grammatical construction; **parallelism** is a form of repetition and often a sound device.
   Example: I am a jealous bird
                I am outdated and useless

all parallelism—the indispensable tools that make a poem a poem, rather than a paragraph or an essay. A poet looks at one thing and sees another.

You can practice seeing twoness through a simple exercise. Look at the world around you with new eyes, eyes that see ordinary objects as something entirely different. For instance, that ballpoint pen isn't a writing utensil; it's a soldier standing ramrod-straight at military attention. That scotch tape dispenser isn't a mundane piece of office equipment; it's a sleigh waiting to be hitched to a horse. Record some of these comparisons in your journal and brainstorm ways to extend them. *How* is the scotch tape dispenser like a sleigh? The shape is similar—which is obvious—but so is the function. Both hold or carry something. When the tape is pulled out of the dispenser, it looks like the reins of a horse's bridle. You get the idea. You may find some of these comparisons perfect for working into poems, especially if they are accurate at both the literal and **figurative** levels. Once you awaken your right brain to the naturalness of seeing intuitive connections, you will find your world overflowing with poetry ideas.

Recently, I was waiting at the airport for my daughter to arrive from Miami. I hadn't seen her in six months, so the anticipation was mounting as her plane pulled alongside the terminal for the passengers to disembark. In a flash of nostalgia, I saw how this expectancy and this arrival were much like her birth twenty-eight years ago. As she was gathering her luggage inside the plane, I was inside the terminal jotting down images. Later that day, I gave her this poem:

Delivery

A jointed umbilical cord stretches
between me in the terminal
and you in the plane.
Twenty-eight years
wash away in a wave
of the same anticipation.
I feel the same
fluttery thrill as you enter
my world;
the same tears form

- - - The **figurative** level of poetry is the symbolic level implied through carefully selected concrete details that carry a deeper meaning.

in your eyes and mine
as you pause and blink
at the lights.
Your red hair shines
as you gather brightness
and deliver yourself
to my arms.

John Elrick saw how a dead romance is like a dead battery. In his first drafts, this insight was mentioned only in one section of the poem. However, after working through several drafts of a much longer poem that seemed to drift off in too many directions, he saw the need to discard any ideas that didn't fit the original comparison. At the suggestion of our workshop, he rewrote the remaining lines in terms of a battery. The result is a tightly crafted poem that is honest on both the literal and figurative levels. Poets call this type of extended metaphor a **poetic conceit:**

Battery

My grip tight
on a greasy wrench,
I connect wires
to the battery.
Sparks fly, electrons flow,
and I feel her
negative energy.

I lose my grip,
fall backwards
into a shelf
where my old battery rests.
"Diehard," it says,
and it did.

I concentrate on pain,
pull myself up,
brandish the wrench.
Inside the hood,
wires red and black,
positive or negative—
my choice.

Electricity flowed all night,
but I hear no sound,
see no sparks,

just cold gray metal marked
"Long Life."
I unplug the charger,
make room on the shelf.
This battery is dead.

☼ FIRESTARTERS

Look into your own life for ideas. How is one thing like another? List five emotions that can be translated into experiences as concrete as John's battery. Record these notes in your journal for future poems.   ☼

Figures of Speech

> "... I am the highway and a peregrine and all the
> sails that ever went to sea."
>
> *Robert James Waller*

Comparison is the backbone of poetry. To clarify or catalog a new idea, we instinctively measure it against something that is already familiar. For example, if I discovered a new flower, I might describe it to you by saying that it is shaped like a daisy, with leaves like a dahlia, and bright colors like a tulip. That's if I am not a poet. If I am a poet, I will describe it in terms unlike itself. I might say that it is shaped like a windmill, with leaves like platters, and colors from a kindergarten paintbox. I am creating images through figures of speech.

A **metaphor** is an indirect comparison, where one thing is presented in terms of another. No comparing words are used. For example:

I am no road for you

An **oxymoron** is a combination of two seemingly opposite terms:

jumbo shrimp
little giant
painful pleasure

A **paradox** is a statement that seems contradictory but is actually true:

Beauty is truth, truth beauty

Personification is a type of metaphor in which an inanimate object is given the qualities of life:

Branches moaned in the wind

A **simile** is a direct comparison where one thing is said to be like another. A comparing word or phrase is used:

His words race through your head like a freight train

When Aaron Anstett took a poetry writing class in his freshman year of college, a member of the class who was obviously new to poetry complained that all of his poems were filled with similes. She said, "I'll bet you couldn't write a poem without similes!" He took her challenge, and for the next workshop, he wrote "A Poem Without Similes," which in a later revision became "when I say chair":

when I say chair

when I say chair
I just mean chair, and not, for instance,
a rainy street in China
or that meatloaf in the refrigerator
you should have thrown out weeks ago.
you can sit down in a poem like this
and relax, because it wouldn't be proper here
for a tulip to pass itself off as an ax handle
or a butcher's smock to pretend
it's anything like an eyelid.
already you've picked up a book
and are turning the pages in a way
that doesn't in the least resemble
hummingbirds caught in the horse's throat
or someone falling from a building.
and now that the night has come on
like the night coming on,
you put the book down
and look out the window:
the stars aren't made of iron
and starting to rust

the stars aren't the dandruff
on a blind man's collar

As you work with figures of speech, you will find that they naturally extend themselves into families of images. This is exactly what you
want: a unifying force that builds intensity. Below, in her poem
"Crows," which was part of her Scholastic Award collection, Brenda
Gregoline extends the metaphor of crows all the way through her poem.
Crows are scavengers: dark, foreboding birds that throughout history
have been symbolic of death. In *Julius Caesar*, Cassius interprets the
presence of "ravens, crows, and kites" flying over his legions as a por-
tent of defeat. Edgar Allan Poe made the raven an indelible symbol of
death in the memories of generations of students when he had his
"raven quoth 'nevermore.'" Brenda draws on this rich legacy when she
makes crows the subject of her poem. However, she takes the metaphor
a step further when she also presents the crows as the black-gowned
judge and jury delivering a sentence of doom:

Crows

On this third day of winter they arrive,
flyers advertising the sale of some dark death.
Refusing to fly south, they choose to bend
my telephone wires and tree branches,
their bodies like heavy leather jackets,
and screech brass all night to keep me awake.
Tonight I climb the hill behind the house
to the crow's court, a judge and jury
balancing my life like a full coffee cup.
They deliver sentence with the shuffling of feathers,
slowly rise, becoming night,
and I feel this dark sky tilt on one wing,
beating danger down around me.

On a sheet of paper list all of the figures of speech using the crow
imagery: metaphor, simile, personification. Which images pertain to traditional images of death and doom; which extend the crow into new
areas? Trace the convergence of the crow metaphors into the last four
lines, as final as a jury sentence.

Are you beginning to wonder how anyone can write a poem without figures of speech? So am I. A poet sees the twoness of things.

☼ FIRESTARTERS

1. Use personification to give life to the following:

  a Dear John letter
  a bad report card
  stale chewing gum
  an empty wallet
  a fat dog

2. Leaf through a volume of poetry or a well-written short story or novel to find five examples each of simile and metaphor. Write them down and take them to class for discussion.

3. Choose one of the similes or metaphors from your list and brainstorm on paper at least five ways it can be extended in the same way Brenda worked with her crow metaphor. Save this exercise in your portfolio to be woven into a poem.   ☼

Symbols

Robert Frost said that a poet "thinks of something in connection with something else that no one ever put with it before." This is Frost's homespun way of saying that poets deal with dual meanings. This is not to say that all poems must be filled with symbols, or that poets are working with a sort of code in order to be obscure. Rather, poets deal with symbols to clarify meaning. They realize that life is experienced through the senses, and that it can be shared with others only through concrete representations of abstractions—in other words, **symbols.** If I say, "I miss you," you have a vague notion of how I feel. If I write, "I am the last patch of winter-gray snow," you experience how lonely I am.

When a poet chooses to deal with symbolism, he is actually writing two poems, one superimposed over the other. Therefore, it is absolutely essential that he remembers that all details of the poem must be literally true before they can be figuratively true. In other words, the concrete, literal level must work before we can even consider the symbolic level. A poem like this begins when a poet sees that one thing is like another.

--- A **symbol** is a concrete representation of an abstract idea. Something that is **concrete** can be felt through the senses. Something that is **abstract** cannot be recognized through the senses.

My son often watches the Saturday morning programs about hunting and fishing. One morning I was working in the next room and overheard the commentary about how to hunt white-tailed mule-deer. It occurred to me that what the narrator was saying about stalking deer also applies to how men stalk women. I began to jot down ideas about the twoness of things. I was careful to record the details of deer hunting exactly as they were related, then applied them later to the human hunt. Here is the poem that revealed itself as I worked:

How to Kill a White Tailed Mule-Deer (with One Shot Straight to the Heart)

You do your killing early,
in the cold damp of morning,
before thermal winds can warn her
of your gun.
She can smell danger at a hundred yards,
in your just-shampooed hair, your musk aftershave,
the scent of your man-sweet skin.
You penetrate her
perimeter of defense slowly, for she's skittish,
with ears alert and hooves
poised to run.
She has known gunshots before.
You stand upwind and wait
until she relaxes her guard;
a white tailed mule-deer may freeze
and listen five minutes or more
for the smallest snap of a twig.
You use a hollow-nosed bullet
designed to mushroom and maim.
It is indelicate and bloody,
but guaranteed this time, to kill.

Out of fairness to my reader and the desire to communicate clearly, I inserted details in lines six and seven that would appeal more to a human female than to a deer, *although they are still literally true for the deer.* It would be unfair of me to write solely in terms of the deer and then expect my reader to make the leap to the human level without assistance.

Ridgely Dunn uses the symbolism of a desert serpent to take her love poem far beyond the usual expectations. Her title "This Metaphor" alerts the reader that this poem is intended to be read at two levels:

This Metaphor

"She's the snake; I'm sure of it."

I've bled an oasis for you.
Standing in the desert,
you throw rocks at fate,
believing I am not the well
you'd want to dip your hands in.
There are monsters here,
sidewinders and the skinless skulls
of luckier beasts.

Would you recognize me
if I blew through the leather flap,
leapt into the flames?
Would you expel me like smoke?
Or do you pretend to dream about me,
tell your comrades
how I eat you inside out with terror?

Within twisted scales, bed sheets,
you gasp, but I strangle.
There are rites of passage involved.
I swallow myself with nightmares.
I could lick your wounds and still taste roses.

Trace the journey of Ridgely's imagery. How is the speaker the snake? How does Ridgely enrich her poem with Middle Eastern desert allusions?

☀ FIRESTARTERS

Divide a sheet of paper into two columns. On the left, list all the nouns in Ridgely's poem; on the right list all the verbs. Circle the words with direct connection to the desert symbolism. Your many circles show how tightly the poem is written and how pervasive Ridgely's symbol has become.

In your own life, take nothing for granted. Begin looking at the world through comparisons. These insights may flower into poems. Record these comparisons, these symbols, in your journal. ☀

SOUND

Flip through the table of contents of a British poetry text, and you are sure to find dozens of poems titled "Song." The popularity of the title is very likely due to the common roots of poetry and song. The earliest poems were accompanied by music and therefore followed the common practices of songwriting: rhythm (meter), rhyme, repetition. Today, while poetry and song are still blood relations, they have moved into different houses. We occasionally hear performance poets who set their poems to music and intend their poems for live performance rather than the page, but the greater percentage of poets commit their words to paper without the embellishment of musical instruments. How can they preserve the sounds of poetry, the most certain means of distinction between poetry and prose? Largely, they rely on the same set of sound devices that have served poets all along.

Alliteration is the repetition of the initial consonant sound or repetition of the same consonant sound in any stressed syllables:

We keep the *w*all between us as *w*e go

Assonance is the repetition of related vowel sounds:

st*a*rs *a*re slowly being born

Cacophony is the use of harsh, unpleasant sounds:

Here we go round the prickly pear

Consonance is the repetition of consonants with changes in the vowel sounds:

dilly-dally

Euphony is the use of melodious, pleasant sounds:

When I am dead, my dearest, sing no sad songs for me

Onomatopoeia is the use of words whose sounds reflect the sounds they describe:

the tintinnabulation of the bells, bells, bells, bells

For what may be the best study in sound ever written, read—and reread—"The Bells" by Edgar Allan Poe. Study which letters and which sounds are emphasized with the various bells, and apply this lesson to your own work. Poe was, of course, experimenting with sound, but he was also matching the sounds to the bells and the situations described in each verse. Even today, poets are conscious of the need to match sound to content:

The Bells

Hear the sledges with the bells,
    Silver bells!
What a world of merriment their melody foretells!
   How they tinkle, tinkle, tinkle,
    In the icy air of night!
While the stars that oversprinkle
All the heavens, seem to twinkle
    With a crystalline delight;
  Keeping time, time, time,
  In a sort of runic rhyme,
To the tintinnabulation that so musically wells
  From the bells, bells, bells, bells,
    Bells, bells, bells—
  From the jingling and the tinkling of the bells.

        II

Hear the mellow wedding bells,
    Golden bells!
What a world of happiness their harmony foretells!
   Through the balmy air of night
   How they ring out their delight!
   From the molten-golden notes,
    And all in tune,
   What a liquid ditty floats
To the turtledove that listens, while she gloats
    On the moon!
  Oh, from out the sounding cells,
What a gush of euphony voluminously wells!
    How it swells!
    How it dwells
  On the future! how it tells

Of the rapture that impels
To the swinging and the ringing
Of the bells, bells, bells,
Of the bells, bells, bells, bells,
Bells, bells, bells—
To the rhyming and the chiming of the bells!

III

Hear the alarum bells,
Brazen bells!
What a tale of terror, now, their turbulency tells!
In the startled ear of night
How they scream out their affright!
Too much horrified to speak,
They can only shriek shriek,
Out of tune,
In a clamorous appealing to the mercy of the fire,
In a mad expostulation with the deaf and frantic fire,
Leaping higher, higher, higher,
With a desperate desire,
And a resolute endeavor
Now—now to sit or never,
By the side of the pale-faced moon.
Ohh, the bells, bells, bells!
What a tale their terror tells
Of despair!
How they clang, and clash, and roar!
What a horror they outpour
On the bosom of the palpitating air!
Yet the ear, it fully knows,
By the twanging
And the clanging,
How the danger ebbs and flows;
Yet the ear distinctly tells,
In the jangling
And the wrangling,
How the danger sinks and swells—
By the sinking or the swelling in the anger of the bells,
Of the bells,
Of the bells, bells, bells, bells,
Bells, bells, bells—
In the clamor and the clangor of the bells!

IV

Hear the tolling of the bells,
    Iron bells!
What a world of solemn thought their monody compels!
    In the silence of the night
    How we shiver with affright
  At the melancholy menace of their tone!
    For every sound that floats
    From the rust within their throats
      Is a groan.
    And the people—ah, the people,
  They that dwell up in the steeple,
      All alone,
    And who tolling, tolling, tolling
    In that muffled monotone,
  Feel a glory in so rolling
      On the human heart a stone—
They are neither man nor woman,
They are neither brute nor human,
     They are ghouls:
    And their king it is who tolls;
  And he rolls, rolls, rolls,
      Rolls
     A paean from the bells;
    And his merry bosom swells
      With the paean of the bells,
    And he dances, and he yells:
    Keeping time, time, time,
In a sort of runic rhyme,
    To the paean of the bells,
      Of the bells:
    Keeping time, time, time,
   In a sort of runic rhyme,
      To the throbbing of the bells,
  Of the bells, bells, bells—
     To the sobbing of the bells;
    Keeping time, time, time,
      As he knells, knells, knells,
  In a happy runic rhyme,
      To the rolling of the bells,
Of the bells, bells, bells:
     To the tolling of the bells,

Of the bells, bells, bells, bells,
   Bells, bells, bells—
To the moaning and the groaning of the bells.

Reread the poem two or three times, studying the length of the verses and the sounds used in them. The first verse is short and crisp: lightly jingling sleigh bells that are reflected both through onomatopoeia—*tinkle, jingle*—and alliteration. Poe chooses sounds that trip easily off the tongue—*t* and *s*—and uses them in words that are as light as the sounds they describe: *oversprinkle, twinkle, jingling, tinkling,* and the wonderful *tintinnabulation.* The second verse is a bit longer to accommodate the slightly heavier metal of the bells. Here the sounds are heavier as well: *m, l,* and *w;* rich, deep sounds that require longer to voice; and words that take full advantage of those sounds: *mellow, molten-golden, harmony, euphony.* In this verse Poe also uses assonance to create a melodious, soothing tone that complements the wedding bells. The third verse is longer still, and the word choices and sounds reflect the frantic scream of alarm bells. Onomatopoeia and cacophony shriek as loudly and harshly as the bells: *clang, clash, roar, twanging, clanging, clamor, clangor, shriek, scream.* The sounds in this verse are equally disturbing: the sharp *c* in *clamor* and the unpleasant intonation of *jangling* and *wrangling.* The fourth, and by far the longest, verse surrounds the heavy tolling of the iron death bell, ghouls of bells, as Poe calls them. He draws out words with the same slow intonation of the bells: *melancholy menace, muffled monotone;* he abruptly closes the ninth line of the stanza with a period following a one-syllable word—*groan*—the only point where he does this in the interior of a verse. The *m* here is not comforting; it is somber: *solemn, monody, menace, muffled;* the *g* is heavy and frightening: *ghouls, groan, groaning.* The onomatopoeia in *tolling* and *throbbing* seems downright threatening, and the internal rhyme of *moaning* and *groaning* weighs down the closure like the iron bell. Some sounds can change their connotations when surrounded by other appropriate sounds. Poets are very aware of the sounds of individual words, phrases, and lines, and how they work together in the poem. As Poe proved so well, sound is inseparable from content.

Among twentieth-century poets, Robert Frost was acutely aware of how sound operates in a poem:

Stopping by Woods on a Snowy Evening

Whose woods these are I think I know
His house is in the village though;

He will not see me stopping here
To watch his woods fill up with snow.

My little horse must think it queer
To stop without a farmhouse near
Between the woods and frozen lake
The darkest evening of the year.

He gives his harness bells a shake
To ask if there is some mistake.
The only other sound's the sweep
Of easy wind and downy flake.

The woods are lovely, dark, and deep,
But I have promises to keep,
And miles to go before I sleep,
And miles to go before I sleep.

Reread Frost's poem and consider the effect of the sound patterns. The lines about the horse are light and quick; they fall easily from the tongue. The horse is impatient to move on. The lines about the man are slower, more contemplative. Note how the vowel sounds, especially the double vowels, slow things down. Try to pronounce *w* or *n* or *l* or *r* or *pr* quickly. You can't do it. Frost is completely in control of pace throughout the poem. Consider how crucial sound is to this poem. Even the inverted words add to the aura: "Whose woods these are I think I know." The line would scan exactly the same with the normal word order: "I think I know whose woods these are," but the sound of poetry would be lost. There is more operating here than meter alone.

In the following poem, Brenda Gregoline shows that she understands sound:

Industrial Seduction

Gears grinding in the night
conforming her body to a different
shape each time.
Finished, he sleeps.
When those eyes are closed, hers
can open.
Until the morning sitting
bruised and egg-shell empty
while he shreds toast with strong white teeth
she breathes coffee vapors and thinks:
How dark is this machine.

Examine this poem carefully; it is short, but it does its job completely. The poem says it all. We know all about this relationship both through the images and through the sound. "Gears grinding" has an unpleasant sound for an unpleasant image. The sounds ". . . he shreds toast with strong white teeth" are as sharp as his teeth and make him seem like a carnivorous animal. Isn't it appropriate that at breakfast the woman feels "egg-shell" empty? And isn't that last line perfect? The letters *w, d, r,* and *m* weight the line down just like a machine.

Remember these tips as you revise your own poems. Read them aloud to yourself and to others as you develop an ear for sound.

☼ FIRESTARTERS

In either a prose paragraph or a poem, conduct your own experiment with sound. Besides the usual sound devices of onomatopoeia and alliteration, try assonance, cacophony, consonance, and euphony; select sounds to match the content of your writing. File this exercise in your portfolio. ☼

POETIC DICTION

Every word in a poem must work with every other word in meaning, tone, and sound. This unity of word choice is called **diction.** When the poet has chosen precisely the right word for the right place, no substitution would work. In the following exercise, you will put yourself into Raymond Carver's mindset as he wrote and revised this poem. Consider the alternatives as carefully as he most certainly did. Whether or not you choose the correct words is unimportant; it is the experience of debating word choices that counts:

At Night the Salmon Move

At night the salmon move
out from the _____ and into town. (river, water)
They avoid places with _____ (signs, names)
like Foster's Freeze, A & W, Smiley's,
but swim close to the _____ (tract, subdivision)
homes on Wright Avenue where sometimes
in the early morning _____ (light, hours)
you can hear them trying doorknobs

or _____ against Cable TV lines. (bumping, hitting)
We wait up for them.
We leave our _____ windows open (upstairs, back)
and call out when we hear a splash.
Mornings are a_____. (disappointment, revelation)

In your workshop circle go through the poem line by line, discussing reasons for each word choice. The idea here is to gain a sense of the nuances of language and to carry over the same careful thought to choosing words for your own poems.

Highlighting Parallel Images

> *"A poem is a thought-felt thing."*
>
> *Robert Frost*

They've been shot, the newscaster says, as pictures of the dead flash on the screen. There are the victims who won't come home from work after sweating in the kitchen heavy with the smells of grease and fried chicken. I mention it at dinner, only to have my mother serve it back with the mashed potatoes. "Not at the table," she says. She shakes her head and passes the carrots. Later, I lie in bed, remembering yearbook pictures on TV, of life pinched out like candle flames. Tonight I know I'll dream of them. My stomach aches, full of food and television. I dream of blood and grease.

Sarah Palomaki was moved and horrified by a senseless mass murder of employees in a local fast food restaurant. Emotion prompted her to write the proceeding journal entry. Even though she knew none of the victims, she felt a personal connection to them. The television newscaster and her mother, however, represent the depersonalization of violence. For whatever reasons, perhaps as a defense against the ugliness of reality, most people do not internalize the tragedies of others. In order to draw this distinction, Sarah knew she needed a more formal package than a journal entry. Each small idea was significant and led naturally into the next. To highlight each image, she placed it in a single line of free verse. The lines roll like gunshots, the subject of her poem.

Notice the impact when the ideas are arranged in free verse. Ideally, each line should present an idea of its own, then enlarge in meaning when coupled with the successive line. Remove all unnecessary words and look for opportunities to achieve parallelism. Reading down the right hand side of the poem should reveal no weak word choices. (The revision history of this poem is detailed in Chapter 6.)

A TV Massacre

They've been shot
the newscaster says
as pictures of the dead
flash on the screen
victims who won't come home
from work after sweating
blood and tears
in the kitchen heavy with smells
of grease and fried chicken

I mention it at dinner
to have it served back with the mashed potatoes
"Not at the table," my mother says,
shakes her head and passes
the carrots

I lie in bed, remembering
yearbook pictures on TV
of life pinched out
like candle flames
Tonight I know I'll dream of them
My stomach aches, full of food
and television
I dream of blood and grease

☼ FIRESTARTERS

Look though your journal for freewritings rich with images and emotion. Follow Sarah's example in arranging your lines into free verse. Once you have established the form, go over the poem relentlessly for unnecessary words and cut them out. Also, search for opportunities to choose strong words to replace weak words or phrases.   ☼

What about Glue Words?

Parts of speech can easily be arranged in order of power:

1. Nouns and verbs

2. Adjectives and adverbs

3. Prepositions, articles, conjunctions—no meaning; just glue

Kathleen Chase shows the power of the right nouns and the right verbs. The spareness of diction gives this poem its power:

Ethereal Whisper

I stand
looking into the past.
Norway Pines chant psalms.
I am mesmerized by the wind
whispering
with a voice as small
as the origin of the Mississippi,
raw
as a new world.
I hear its tale of
subjugation and sorrow
proclaiming this ground
hallowed.

In the following example, I have rewritten Luis Hernandez's tightly constructed poem into a poem sticky with glue. By placing the two versions side by side, the difference is apparent: the deadening effect of weak "being" verbs, conjunctions, and redundant words destroys the poem on the left. Remember: it is not the subject you choose to write about that makes your poem successful; it is the skill with which you write it. Poets pare away flabby language wherever it appears. Much of the power of poetry comes from its intense, concise diction. Don't lose your poem in rolls of fat:

There isn't any corn

There isn't any corn for the crows
this late in the fall season
we race by these fields that look
like golden blurs
This gold is the color of ending
It is the color of October
We roll up the windows
to avoid the chill outside the car
and between the two of us

no corn for the crows

no corn for the crows
this late in the season
we race by these fields,
golden blurs
this color of ending
this color of october,
with windows rolled up
to avoid the chill
outside
and between us

✵ FIRESTARTERS

Go over poems you have written for previous exercises and tighten them
like a guitar string. Only the right note will do.   ✵

The Right Word in the Right Place

I am the woodpile
And you are a match
But we've got to watch out:
Flames can burn us

I am the tinder
You are the spark
But we must be wary:
Flames burn

Instinct probably tells you that the poem on the left is much stronger
than that on the right even though both express the same idea. Diction
makes the difference. *Tinder* is more accurate and specific than *woodpile;* besides, who would want to be called a woodpile? It's just not poetic. *Spark* fits the context of a love poem much better than *match,* and
wary is both more interesting and specific than *watch out. Flames burn*
finishes the poem abruptly and strongly; it *sounds* like a warning.
Flames can burn us sounds like a nursery school teacher. As poets we
must be ruthless in holding ourselves responsible for each word, for
considering carefully whether it is, indeed, the best word.

When you are writing or revising poems, experiment with word
order; position words to emphasize meaning and sound:

The green grapes
you dangled before
Tantalus were very sweet.
But they remain beyond reach
forever, like you.

So sweet
the green, green grapes
you dangled before Tantalus.
But like you they remain forever
beyond reach.

Why is the cinquain on the right more pleasing? In the first place, the lines are more balanced; you can see that on the page. Also, moving *so sweet* to the opening line creates alliteration as well as highlights the subject of the poem, the lure of the lover. *Green, green grapes* again is alliterative, and the repetition works for emphasis. The *green, green* seems sensuously tantalizing. Word order is crucial in building to the closure. The point here is that the lover is forever *beyond reach*, so those words belong in the last line. Finally, your poet's ear should tell you that the order of words in the cinquain on the right is metrically more pleasing than the prosaic word order on the left. In revising your own work, keep in mind that you may have chosen the right words; you may simply need to shift their order.

☼ FIRESTARTERS

Look through poems you have written for assignments or recorded in your journal and hold yourself to the strictest truth telling. Can some words be replaced with more accurate choices? Can some be eliminated entirely? Can some be moved to more appropriate positions? Would the sound of the poem improve if you were to shift some constructions? Add the revisions to your working portfolio. This is how poets work; they return again and again to the same pieces, each time looking at them with a different eye.   ☼

Writer's Secret: Using Nouns as Verbs

Read the poem that follows, "Garage Sale," by Lucien Stryk. Like other successful writers, he is selective in all word choices, especially nouns and verbs. In poetry, even more than prose, verb choices are crucial. Serious writers learn early to use strong, metaphorical verbs, words that create images in the reader's mind. Astute writers adapt nouns to use as verbs on just the right occasions. Since nouns generally create both mind pictures and sensory associations, they can serve double purposes as verbs. Read the third verse of "Garage Sale" carefully; *lynx*, acting as a verb, brings exactly the right image to the situation. Consider how lame the mundane verb *look* would seem in its place. What qualities of a lynx does Stryk see in the eyes of the garage sale critic? By using the verb *lynx*, these qualities are seen as part of the image; he does not have to verbalize them:

Garage Sale

. . . so the nightmare enters
where I wait the rummagers

hunched in a beat-up lawnchair,
feet astride the oil-smudge

on the floor. A car pulls up,
a critic's eyes lynx through

the windshield and the motor
churns, roars off. Well,

I'm just a jingler sharing
the dust with spiders, come

with over sixty years of
misplaced images, not everybody's

bargain. A white-haired couple
drop in, regard me with suspicion—

what a pity I am not their long
lost son. Take me, I say. Come

buy nothing for nothing, poems
thrown in free. As they fade out

I take the garage sale sign
down, hope for a better day.

☼ FIRESTARTERS

1. Look over some of your own journal writings or other pieces in your portfolio, and try your hand at adapting nouns into verbs. Below is a list of some examples. You will surely think of many others.

ferret	jackknife
rubberband	finger
ribbon	flake
string	frost
pen/pencil	screen
soldier	whip
spike	wrinkle
puddle	ruffle
people (populate)	squirrel
tower	peak
bike	skate

wire	meter
monitor	clog
snake	badger
wolf	house
venom	pearl

Caution: Draw on your vocabulary, your thesaurus, or your dictionary to find *exactly* the right word. Often, verbs may have the same root and be similar in meaning, but one will feel more right than the others. Example: *satisfy, satiate, sate.* Now substitute some of these new, stronger verbs for weak verbs in an early piece of writing.

2. Write ten original sentences using nouns as verbs. Underline your verbs. You may borrow from the list above, or even better, think of some of your own. When you are finished, circle your favorite, then go around the workshop, allowing each writer to read a sentence.

THE IMAGIST LEGACY

Although most modern free verse would not be considered imagist by the strictest definition of the term, its genealogy continues to show imagist ancestry. Along with sound, imagery continues to define poems today. Many free verse poems still present the reader with a bold juxtaposition of images leading to an intuitive connection. The following exercise will take you through the steps necessary to create an abrupt collision of images that lead, without transition, to illumination.

Linking the Ordinary and the Unexpected

A poem, like a story, needs to have a sense of setting, character, and movement. It should begin with concrete details that broaden into a distinct closure. Follow these directions, and the restrictions will provide you with a free verse poem that works:

1. Choose a routine task in your life to begin the framework. Write one or two lines.

2. Introduce an incident that disrupts your routine and balloons in importance. This incident must contrast sharply with the mundane nature of your task. Write four to eight lines.

3. Return without transition to your original task. Write one to two lines.

The collision of the ordinary and the unexpected should create an aura that lingers beyond the closing lines:

Correction

Red pen in hand,
I bow over their essays—

The phone rings;
his voice talks
toneless, flat,
then stops abruptly.
For fifteen beats of a heart
I freeze.
I replace the receiver
and arrange my face.

I grade the papers.
                    Carol Morrison

Steam

Steam rises from the tea
to warm my lips.

A deer, frozen
against snow stares
through the glass at my
bare face. Wind cracks through
branches breaking it free,
streaking toward shelter.

I breathe waves
into my tea, steam rises.
                    Sheryl Sullivan

Note the sharp interplay of warmth and cold that heighten the contrast and provide the framework for Sheryl's poem. In your journal, jot down a list of the nouns and verbs in this poem. Through working with the restricted syllables and careful word choices required by short forms, Sheryl learned that the right nouns and verbs rarely need modifiers.

Using Tercets in Free Verse

Peter Noback uses tercets in his free verse to create a balanced appearance on the page, an aesthetic sense of control, and a carefully considered selection of sound devices, including assonance, alliteration, repetition, and meter. My assignment asked the students to extend their line lengths to approximate blank verse. The longer lines add substance and richness to the poem and create a pleasing unity of form.

Peter had already worked his way through several early drafts before he gave me this poem. In the text that follows you will see the first draft he submitted to me, his comments and mine, and its final form. Peter had learned that free verse succeeds when the poet knows how to choose the right form and restrictions for his or her subject:

Waves

I love this poem!

These mornings blow cold off the lake
through the screen and boards of the porch.
I swallow them like a sore throat.

I rise early, hot tea in hand, chained
to the sunrise carried to me across the water
with the rise and fall of the waves.

I've tried to establish a thread of breathing and its movement (underlined), but I'm not sure if it works. (P.N.)

The rooms of the house are as still
as my breathing and these empty spaces inhale
the morning light and the dust upon the shelf.

Down by the pier, a sailboat's rusted chains
shackle it to the shore and the mast pole
(has) no hoisted sail to block the vast blue.

wc

Later today, (I'll bait my fishing lure,)
anchor my legs over the edge
of the dock as I cast and wait,

Not exactly accurate. A lure is bait.

grow tired and retreat barefoot up the path
back to the sunken wooden house,
rows of Frank Lloyd Wright window panes

the trees breathe through. I'll fall asleep
on the wicker swing after a sandwich and chips,
a (parched) book rises and falls on my chest.

Can a book be "parched"?

The only sound, the creaking of this house,
the rhythm of each sweeping wave.

My first reaction was that this could be a prize-winning poem. (He did become a finalist in the Portfolio Category in the Scholastic Writing

Awards.) Among his many fine images and lines, two are especially startling in their originality:

I swallow them like a sore throat.

   and

rows of Frank Lloyd Wright window panes
the trees breathe through. I'll fall asleep

I also liked the way he carries ideas over from one tercet to the next rather than settling for a succession of end-stopped lines. His stanzas move as gently as the waters he writes about.
 Here is the final revision:

Waves

These mornings blow cold off the lake
through the screen and boards of the porch.
I swallow them like a sore throat.

I rise early, hot tea in hand, chained
to the sunrise carried to me across the water
with the rise and fall of the waves.

The rooms of the house are as still
as my breathing and these empty spaces inhale
the morning light and the dust upon the shelf.

Down by the pier, a sailboat's chains rust,
shackled to the shore and the mast pole,
no hoisted sail flapping against the vast blue.

Later today, I'll fasten my fishing lure,
anchor my legs over the edge of the dock,
toes dry above the water as I cast and wait,

grow tired and retreat barefoot up the path
back to the wooden house sunk into the hill,
rows of Frank Lloyd Wright window panes

the trees breathe through. I'll fall asleep
on the wicker swing after a sandwich and chips,
a brittle book rising and falling on my chest.

The only sound, the creaking of this house,
the rhythm of each sweeping wave.

In writing about his grandmother's house on the shore of Lake Michigan, Peter wanted to show how the house has become still, a place for relaxation and solitude. Which images show oldness? Which show lack of action? Which show the pull of comfort and tranquillity? Peter uses assonance, the repetition of vowel sounds and soft consonants—*r, w, f, d, m*— to lull his reader into the same contemplative mood he feels. Poet Steven Dunn, quoted on page 194, would approve of the merging here of subject and craft.

☼ FIRESTARTERS

Write your own free verse poem using tercets and lines between seven and eleven syllables in length to describe a place you know well. Choose your sound devices carefully to recreate the scene. Try to carry some of the lines over from one tercet to the next to create a smooth flow and unity.   ☼

CHAPTER 5

LIGHTING THE FIRE:

Poems from Models

❝It is essential that these logs be well bedded down in the ash as the point is to keep the flames and draft out from under the logs so only their tops and faces burn.**❞**

Raymond W. Dyer,
The Old Farmer's Almanac

> *"Hemingway studied, as models, the novels of*
> *Knut Hamsun and Ivan Turgenev. Isaac Bashevis*
> *Singer, as it happened, also chose Hamsun and Tur-*
> *genev as models. Ralph Ellison studied Hemingway*
> *and Gertrude Stein. Thoreau loved Homer; Eudora*
> *Welty loved Chekhov. Faulkner described his debt to*
> *Sherwood Anderson and Joyce; E. M. Forster, his debt*
> *to Jane Austen and Proust. By contrast, if you ask a*
> *twenty-one-year-old poet whose poetry he likes, he*
> *might say, unblushing, 'Nobody's.' In his youth he has*
> *not yet understood that poets like poetry, and novelists*
> *like novels; he himself likes only the role, the thought*
> *of himself in a hat."*
>
> *Annie Dillard*, The Writing Life

Lucien Stryk tells us that poetry requires a twenty-year apprenticeship. He is not alone in that belief. *The Morrow Anthology of Younger American Poets* features those poets under age forty-five who are considered by that publisher to be at the forefront of their generation of "new" poets. Does this news seem disheartening to you? It shouldn't. Actually, it can be reassuring to know that no one expects you to be "mature" as a poet until you have lived and read poetry for another twenty years.

You may wonder, however, just what are you supposed to be doing while you read poetry and practice your art? You will be writing, of course, all the time, and your writing will naturally reflect the influence of some of the poets you read. As you read, both consciously and unconsciously you will be absorbing each poet's "bag of tricks" and incorporating them into your own. You may expect your voice as a poet to evolve as you continue to read and study. Eventually, your own voice will be the essence of who you are plus the aesthetic influence of all the poets you have read. That is why it is so important to read and study poets who are good and who are setting the standard for poetry today. In this chapter you will find lessons built around some of those poets. The lessons will help you learn how to break down and analyze what each poet does and incorporate those techniques into your own work. In other words, these lessons will allow you to try on a showroom of other poets' clothes and see how they fit. Those that suit you best will turn up later in your own wardrobe.

POEMS THAT RIDE THE BUS: A Model by Ruth Forman

Ruth Forman's first book of poems, *We Are the Young Magicians,* follows the advice she gives about poetry in the following poem. She writes honest and memorable poems about real people in the language real people speak. Her poems are set in schoolrooms, on the front steps of a Philadelphia tenement building, on the hot summer streets of her neighborhood. The people are the boys who shoot baskets in the school yard, the first grader who wets her pants, the girls who braid their hair in cornrows and wish they were grown up. Her poems are written for them and for you, the real people who go to school, dream summer dreams, and ride the bus.

Poetry Should Ride the Bus

poetry should hopscotch in a polka dot dress
wheel cartwheels
n hold your hand
when you walk past the yellow crack house

poetry should wear bright red lipstick
n practice kisses in the mirror
for all the fine young men with fades
shootin craps around the corner

poetry should dress in fine plum linen suits
n not be so educated that it don't stop in
every now n then to sit on the porch
and talk about the cumins and goins of the world

poetry should ride the bus
in a fat woman's Safeway bag
between the greens n chicken wings
to be served with Tuesday's dinner

poetry should drop by a sweet potato pie
ask about the grandchildren
n sit through a whole photo album
on a orange plastic covered La-Z-Boy with no place to go

poetry should sing red revolution love songs
that massage your scalp
and bring hope to your blood
when you think you're too old to fight

yeah
poetry should whisper electric blue magic
all the years of your life
never forgettin to look you in the soul
every once in a while
n smile

Try taking Ruth Forman's idea a step further in a poem of your own. Instead of saying that poetry *should* ride the bus, show that it *does* ride the bus and does all of the other things that people do every day. In the following example, I show poetry riding the bus in the shapes of all the people you might see there. Each stanza shows a different person and describes him or her specifically, not only through sight, but *through the other senses* as well. Such imagery is the basis of *imag*ination and of all poetry.

Poetry rides the bus

Poetry rides the bus
and carries a shopping bag.
It rolls its stockings
down to its knees
and wears shoes
with the toes cut out.
It sits next to a window
and talks to itself.

Poetry rides the bus
and carries a briefcase.
It wears dark suits,
conservative ties,
and keeps its wingtips polished.
It stands near the door
and reads *The Wall Street Journal.*

Poetry rides the bus
and carries a shoulder bag.
It sprays its hair into spikes
straight as the spinal armor
of a stegosaurus.
Poetry sits with its girlfriends,
giggles, and cracks its gum.

Poetry rides the bus
and carries a boombox.
It wears a starter jacket,
Air Jordans, and talks
raw rap. It sprawls
sideways in its seat
and drinks soda,
nods coolly to the beat and its friends.

Poetry drives the bus
and sits tall in the seat.
It takes tokens and passes
and lets its friends ride free.
Poetry opens its doors
with a smooth hydraulic hiss
and fits everyone comfortably
into a favorite seat.
Yeah.
          Dedicated to Ruth Forman

If you read through each stanza again carefully, you will see that poetry
can be found in all of the people who ride the bus, *including you*. Poetry will let you ride free and put you comfortably into your favorite seat.
There are as many kinds of poems as there are people on a bus; you will
just need to look around a bit to find the ones you are comfortable with.

☼ FIRESTARTERS

Write your own poem based on Ruth Forman's model. You may wish to
follow my pattern and show—through imagery—poems riding the bus.
Or, you may decide to show poetry doing any of the things people do.
You will probably want to follow Forman's lead in talking about poetry
as if it's a person: in other words, you will use personification.

Here are some things you might find poetry doing in your own
neighborhood. Use this list as a starter, then add your own ideas. Make
this truly your poem by painting images straight from your own life! As
I did, you may wish to dedicate your poem to Ruth Forman, since she
gave us the wonderful image of poetry riding a bus.

going to a ball game	going to a beauty shop
going to school	cooking dinner
driving cars/trucks	driving a taxi
going on a field trip	washing clothes

playing musical instruments	singing
writing rap	coloring balloons
traveling	sightseeing in your town
getting a haircut	buying clothes
drinking soda	telling stories
flying	playing sports

PERFORMANCE POETRY BY DAVID HERNANDEZ

David Hernandez, recognized as the unofficial poet laureate of Chicago, is one of the most widely known performance poets today and certainly one of the pioneers of this new art form. Like other performance poets, Hernandez felt that poetry had become lost to the average person and been made the property of scholars in ivory towers. He decided to reinstate poetry as the voice of Everyone, just as it had been in the past. To do this, he returned to the origins of poetry as oral language and composed poems intended for public performance, often with his band Street Sounds. In the tradition of ancient bards, Hernandez recites richly narrative poems to the musical background of salsa, reggae, country, rock, and other appropriate sounds. However, despite the artistry of the music, it is Hernandez's compelling voice that carries the performance.

David Hernandez's subjects are as varied as his life, and all are lifted directly from his own triggering town, Chicago, where almost everyone is from someplace else. Hernandez immigrated from Puerto Rico as a child, but his subjects are universal. He draws upon childhood memories and old neighborhoods to become a voice for all immigrants when he writes of family, lovers, neighbors, friends, foods, even his dog. Those of us born in the United States are caught up in his poems and brought to a clearer understanding of the immigrant experience; after all, as the old saw reminds us, we are a nation of immigrants. Accordingly, Hernandez's first cassette of performance poems was titled *Immigrants*. Since that time he has brought out two more cassettes and a **chapbook**. Below are three poems from *Elvis Is Dead But At Least He's Not Gaining Any Weight*. Even on the page, without the background of street sounds or the metrical lilt of Hernandez's voice, you will hear the sounds of performance poetry and relive with the poet crystallized moments from his own experience:

--- A **chapbook** is a small collection of poems, usually between twenty and thirty pages, that is printed in soft cover.

Armitage Street

Waiting for the elevated train
during a pale afternoon
I looked down on Armitage Street
full of quaint old buildings
up-scale stores and fashionable mothers
pushing white-walled baby carriages
on well-heeled sidewalks.
        And to think.
It seems just like yesterday on Armitage Street
that Alfredo and Cha-Cha played hide & seek
with Quinto the cop while Cosmo & Aidita
made love in the gangway,
     When radios blared out open windows
     dressed in five & dime lace curtains.
        When staccato Spanish bounced between
       buildings high above the rolling traffic
    because telephones were insultingly impersonal
      & it was no secret that the eyes
      expressed the heart.
When rice and bean smells
roamed the hallways covering up
the tracks of other ethnics who had
since faded into the American Dream.
     When candles danced amber hue
     in roach sprayed apartments
     from all-night vigils for the dead
     before being shipped back home
     in a self-addressed, stamped coffin.
     And the children kissed their cold cheeks
     for all the candy, stories, pony rides,
     and the dead knew they would be missed.
       When 25 cent haircuts at Don Benjamin's
       non-licensed basement barber shop
       made you smell pretty doused in
       Brilliantine hair tonic.
And Nereida,
the beautiful cousin that you
secretly loved, was the official
translator for school teacher notes
pinned to our lapels on coats because
the mothers were all Englishless.

When the last summer days
were spent under rainbow-
hydrant showers and that night
you overheard your parents
talk about moving out again
because the rent was going up.
But you didn't care because last year during school
Ms. Greenspan said that you were a great writer,
Renee kissed you during recess and that was enough
for a whole lifetime. And to think.
It seems just like yesterday
on Armitage Street.

Hernandez even makes poetry out of the simple act of cooking:

Puerto Rice N' Beans

In making Puerto Rice n' Beans
you must live alone after futile
attempts at normality.
Your ex-lovers still send birthday cards
because you were such a roller coaster
and though they are presently very happy
with their significant others, they always
remember you when things get monotonous.
Make sure it is a quiet Friday night
with hissing steam heaters working full-time,
and that there is nothing happening
but the craving for rice & beans
like momi cooked every day forever.
So with childhood recipe intact
you boil and simmer the concoction
as you relax in your favorite chair
waiting for the smoke alarm to jerk you
out of slumber because you passed out
once again
Open the windows for the burnt smell to escape
and anticipate your neighbor's comments about
that crazy Rican barbecuing rice & beans again.
Call a dear friend
with a working car
and invite them to dinner
at the San Juan Restaurant.

Then you order fish & plantanos
because you lost your taste
for rice and beans.
Besides,
you might just get it right
come next Friday night.

The assassination of Dr. Martin Luther King, Jr. changed Hernandez's
life and caused him to take up his pen as a weapon instead of his gun:

Martin and My Father

Martin was too peaceful for me.
He let those Deep-South dogs bite him
Police club his head
Suburbanites stone him
Cowards bomb his house
Firemen hose him down
and judges throw him in jail.

I used to pack a .357 Magnum
and if nobody messed with me,
I would aim, pull the trigger
and feel the kick of the gun
saturated in spic anger.
I wanted to kill all the
racist pigs in the world,
and marching peacefully
like Martin did, wasn't
about to do it.

One time while arguing with my father
I pulled a knife on him.
That night he cried himself to sleep
and I felt like an assassin.
The next day I heard that Martin
was shot dead and my heart crumbled
for him and my father.

My anger turned ice-blue hot,
well-kept, on target,
proportionately forever and
it was on this anvil that
my pen was forged

So I took my gun and knife,
threw them in the lake
and watched them drown.
Then I went home and while
my father took a nap on the couch
with the t.v. blaring about
Martin's death,
I kissed him with a poem.

And I'll tell you,
     That Martin,
          He was something else.

☼ FIRESTARTERS

Look into your own life, your own neighborhood, your own family recipes to find the material for poems. Your success will come from being as honest and concrete as David Hernandez.

Then comes the difference: for this assignment you will need to write a **narrative poem.** It can be a small and gentle story, as in "Puerto Rice N' Beans," or a moment of **epiphany,** as in "Martin And My Father"; or you may simply wish to recreate the neighborhood of your childhood, as in "Armitage Street." In keeping with the narrative approach, you will need to pay very close attention to all the sound devices at your disposal, especially meter. While you may not work with a strict metrical pattern, you will choose your words carefully for sound. Before you begin writing, you may wish to review the lesson on sound. ☼

CHILDREN'S VOICES BY GWENDOLYN BROOKS

No living poet has touched more lives through poetry than Gwendolyn Brooks, Consultant in Poetry to the Library of Congress and Poet Laureate of Illinois. In 1950 she became the first African American to win a Pulitzer Prize, perhaps the most significant of her many awards and

---

- - - A **narrative** poem tells a story.

- - - An **epiphany** is an enlightenment.

honors. She has published many books of poetry, both for adults and children, and has taught poetry widely, ranging from prestigious universities to the Chicago City Jail. Each June she selects several young poets from Illinois schools to receive her Poet Laureate Award at a ceremony she hosts personally at The University of Chicago.

Gwendolyn Brooks believes that poetry should belong to the people; it should reflect their lives, dreams, concerns, and problems. She also believes that poetry should be written in the voices of real people: her own and others'. Reflecting her deep concern for children, especially victimized children, Gwendolyn Brooks recently published *Children Coming Home*, poems written in the individual voices of twenty children on their way home from school. The poems reflect the gamut of their lives: at home, at school, in their hopes, and in their imaginations. Some are warm, like Novelle's contented voice in "My Grandmother Is Waiting For Me To Come Home"; some are deeply disturbing, as Merle's worried voice in "Uncle Seagram"; but all are candid, true, and absolutely convincing. The children speak with children's words, naiveté, and, occasionally, the heartbreaking directness of an abused child. *Children Coming Home* reflects the clarity with which children understand what matters in their individual worlds.

Nineteen Cows in a Slow Line Walking

When I was five years old
I was on a train.
From a train window I saw
nineteen cows in a slow line walking.

Each cow was behind a friend.
Except for the first cow,
who was God.

I smiled until
one cow near the end
jumped in front of a friend.

That reminded me of my mother and my father.
It spelled what is their Together.

I was sorry for the spelling lesson.

I turned my face from the glass.
                                        Jamal

To Be Grown Up

The whole chocolate cake can be yours.

To be grown up means
you don't get a report card.
You don't face a father, a mother.

The walls of the cage are gone.
The fortress is done and down.

To be grown up means
the Bill will be paid by you.

To be grown up means
you can get sick and stay sick.
Your legs will not love you. They'll fail.

No icy sidewalks for sliding.

No grandmother to fix you big biscuits.
No grandfather to sing you "Asleep in the Deep."

Aron

The children speak with the words and directness of real children. The limits of their worlds are apparent: "No icy sidewalks for sliding" and "No grandmother to fix you big biscuits." However, they are capable of deep insight: "That reminded me of my mother and my father." Gwendolyn Brooks shows real artistry in her restraint; she allows the children to speak for themselves and trusts her readers to draw the right conclusions. She knows that a deeply involved reader doesn't mind a little work.

Gwendolyn Brooks has always been a favorite poet among my students, so when we invited her to read at our school, we prepared a booklet of original poems honoring *Children Coming Home.* Each of my students wrote a poem in the voice of a child. Tracy Blight patterned her poem after a boy she had known in grade school:

Phillip

The only Black in our class is
Phillip
but sometimes I forget
that he's Black.
On the wall there's a picture of a stork

with a pink baby girl
because Lisa got a sister last week.
Phillip looks like a stork to me.
His legs are long and make angles
at the knees.
For Black History Month we learned
about Martin Luther King
who was Good
and we listened to his speech
about Dreams;
but Dr. King doesn't sound like Phillip.
His words are wet,
like many black rivers
that run together.

Vanessa Ruppert wrote about a grandmother with osteoporosis:

Grandma Alma

Grandma Alma is ninety years old.
I am almost nine.
She is my mama's grandma.
Each time I visit
the space between hugs
is smaller.
I am growing fast as a dandelion
but she is shrinking
like grapes in the sun.
Her teeth come out at night
and swim in a glass next to her bed.
Oz-tea-oh-poor-oh-sis Mama says.
I wonder if it hurts.
Drink your milk
Mama orders.
I know that Grandma
didn't always finish hers.
Between gulps I look
at the black and white pictures
on the kitchen table,
at Grandma's shiny teeth,
at how tall and straight
she used to stand.

Alice Lee calls back her own childhood in her poem about eating *kim-chee,* Chinese cabbage:

Kim-Chee Basketball

I tried to cut in half
With my chopsticks
My big slice of *kim-chee.*
I sat on my legs;
I poked the pointy ends
Into the middle
And pushed out.
The half piece flew
Into my brother's cup.
I watched the *kim-chee*
Turn lighter
As spicy red stuff
Floated to the top
Of the water.
I closed my mouth,
Looked up to my brother's face.
He laughed,
Then everyone laughed
And said I had invented
A new game.
KIM-CHEE BASKETBALL.
I laughed too.

☀ FIRESTARTERS

Look around at your own world and the children you know well, or draw on your own childhood for inspiration. List memories, beliefs, or concerns. Keep the ideas small: remember, the small situation can represent a larger picture. Close your eyes and return to the words and thought patterns of childhood. Use your senses as a child does: see, hear, touch, taste, smell; life is very concrete for a child. Write a poem in the voice of a child or of yourself when you were much younger. Follow Gwendolyn Brooks's example of presenting a situation simply and frankly; allow your reader the delight of reading between the lines. Read each draft aloud to listen for a child's voice. If possible, read the poem to your workshop for comments. It is both challenging and effective to write in a voice younger than your own.   ☀

CHICANA POEMS BY ANA CASTILLO

Born in Chicago to a father who had been a member of the Toltec street gang, Ana Castillo herself is a fighter—for women's rights and Chicana rights—and her poetry is her best weapon. Her collection *My Father Was a Toltec* chronicles her childhood in a Spanish-speaking neighborhood where the adults clung to the old ways and their children either suffered from discrimination or grew tough in the streets. Ana Castillo grew tough. Even education, that "great equalizer" of humankind, failed Chicano children, as Castillo explores in the following poem:

Red Wagons
c. 1958

in grammar school primers
the red wagon
was for children
pulled along
past lawns on a sunny day.
Father drove into
the driveway. "Look,
Father, look!"
Silly Sally pulled Tim
on the red wagon.

Out of school,
the red wagon carried
kerosene cans
to heat the flat.
Father pulled it to the gas
station
when he was home
and if there was money.

If not, children went to bed
in silly coats
silly socks; in the morning
were already dressed
for school.

Most of us are well aware that Sally, Dick, and Jane did not reach out to any community other than middle-class, white suburbia. Father's neat crew cut and authoritative briefcase and mother's brisk housedress clearly marked their gender roles, and children never went to bed fully dressed in order to keep warm. Father drove a station wagon and lived in a spacious white frame house; he didn't pull a red wagon to the gas station for kerosene to heat his apartment. The cultural gulf between school and home was made painfully apparent to even the youngest Chicano children. Rather than lecture to us about something we already know, Castillo shows us in her poetry exactly what she learned at school.

The life of the Chicana woman was harder even than for the Chicano man. In addition to the incessant pressure of adapting to a foreign language and culture, working outside the home, and doing all the housework inside the home, she had to contend with being a second-class citizen in her own culture. In most Hispanic families, Castillo shows us, the woman bore great hardships, and, like Zoila Lopez, she often developed great fortitude:

Zoila Lopez

If i were you, Zoila,
i wouldn't be here
in English class
with the disturbed child
who sits in the back
with the husband
who doesn't work.
i wouldn't laugh, Zoila,
if my first winter up north
were without boots
and the only thing to
warm me was the photograph
of Jorgito dressed as a
little indian in white
pajamas and sandals on
Guadalupe's Day, just before
he was killed by a truck
that carried oranges.
i wouldn't bathe, change
my dress, look for work,
hold a pencil upright
after this summer when
the baby ran a high fever
and the hospital people in
that marbles-in-the-mouth
language said, "It's okay.

Take her home."
She died that night.
You'd thought she'd just
stopped crying.

i would die, if i were you,
Zoila, a million deaths at
the end of each nightmarish day
with its minuscule hopes like
snowflakes that melt on one's
teeth and tongue and taste of
nothing.

What is it that keeps Zoila Lopez chasing each transitory hope? Is it some warrior spirit inherited from a Toltec ancestor? More likely it is the simple knowledge that her family will disintegrate if she falters. The strength of women like Zoila Lopez is a cross-cultural miracle. No matter what our ethnic backgrounds, we are likely to find accounts of women like her in immigrants from our own family trees.

☼ FIRESTARTERS

One thing we all know for certain is that we are the children of immigrants. In most families we need go back only a generation or two or three before we discover accounts of those brave ancestors who trusted everything they had to an unknown life in an unknown country. Whether we are Hispanic, African American, Irish, or Japanese in our origins, our families at some point all shared the experience of being newcomers to this vast country.

Do some family research: talk to your parents, grandparents, aunts and uncles; do a lot of listening. Uncover names and details and family stories about those ancestors who made the terrifying decision to immigrate. Some may have come legally, some illegally; some may even have been brought unwillingly as slaves; all have their stories to tell. Why did they emigrate? What changes did life in the United States require of them? What were they willing to sacrifice in order to survive? Even if your family is unable to give you much help with your family history, or if you are not living with your birth family and are therefore unable to trace the family tree, you can still complete this assignment. Just go to the library and look at a book containing photographs of immigrants or read about Ellis Island, the New York port through which millions of immigrants passed on their way to a new life. Then use your imagination and your five senses to see, hear, touch, taste, and smell life in the new country. Use the model of "Zoila Lopez" to bring the details of one immigrant's life into focus. To add immediacy and a stronger personal connection, you may wish to use a literary device called **apostrophe** and address the person by name, as Castillo does in her poem.

If, like Ana Castillo, you have a firsthand experience in your own life to draw from, you may choose to model a poem after "Red Wagon." Have you been a "minority" in class? Have you learned English as a second language? Have you felt that history books leave out information about your ethnic group or treat it unfairly? Have you felt out of place or unwelcome in class? Did the characters and stories from elementary school primers seem as foreign as another planet? Here is your opportunity to put discomfort, even pain, to good use. Hold back any impulse to scold or lecture your reader; that is not the province of poetry. Just *show* the experience clearly in the simple language of a child; allow your readers to live in the poem and trust them to feel as you do. They will, if you have done your job as a poet. ☼

FROM ONE'S OWN WORLD: Poems by Frank Lamont Phillips

Like many fine writers of the past few decades, Frank Lamont Phillips was first recognized by the Scholastic Writing Awards, where he won an honorable mention for his poetry. While still in college, his work was included in a widely read anthology, *American Negro Poetry*, edited by the late Arna Bontemps. Phillips writes simple but eloquent poems about people he knows and understands well. He knows that the best poems are already there, in the poet's own life, waiting quietly to be recognized.

Genealogy

The magnolia tress
that blossom in summer sun
on summer days
in the south
have my mother's name

- - - **Apostrophe** in poetry is a device in which an absent person is addressed by the author.

written on each leaf
where her hands
touched saplings that tore
my back
long ago in summer heat
after day
when mama bent
over cotton plant
and sang
in fields where her
mama had worked
before she was born
and had sung
songs too
full of grief for tears

Phillips looks back with love and empathy at two women who had toiled long hours and suffered private griefs so that children like him could prosper. Through concrete imagery, he draws the reader into experiencing the heavy-scented beauty of the magnolia trees he associates with his mother, then moves in the unsettling direction of the cotton fields where his mother labored on scorching summer days. Both are accurate portrayals of the South and of his mother. Their juxtaposition in the same poem and without a stanza break says something about our complacent acceptance of the lives of these women and their sisters. Note the perfect line break at the end of the poem: "and had sung/songs too/full of grief for tears." What a poignant way to show his grandmother singing her grief, probably in the same spirituals her mother and her mother's mother had sung as well.

Maryuma

at seventeen your
thoughts were younger
than your face
and your smile
mirrored in dishwater
was mississippi pleasant
you had large eyes
and larger hopes of marrying
somebody rich
or famous or something
you settled for a little house

so close to the tracks
that the sound of a train shook
some of everything
you settled for a boy
with eyes larger than
your own
you settled for dishwater
just as deep
as that you knew
at home

All of us have known scores of Maryumas. Most of the girls we knew in school have chosen or are on the way to choosing the same fate. What happens to those dreams and smiles of seventeen? How do they become lost in a lifetime of dishwater? Why do the Maryumas settle for so little? Wisely, the poet does not attempt to answer these questions. However, Phillips raises questions in his reader's mind, connecting Maryuma to all the girls like her in the reader's background, and, inevitably, the reader begins to look for answers. Phillips resists the temptation to preach, to blame society, to comment on gender roles within his culture, or to pose as an authority in a field outside his own. He trusts his poem to draw readers in, prompt them to ask questions, and even look for answers.

☼ FIRESTARTERS

Using either "Genealogy" or "Maryuma" as a model, write from inside your own world, from what you know. Look at the people close to you and search for connections between the generations. Choose the appropriate imagery to connect the generations. Or model your poem after "Maryuma," where you will be examining a type of person along with an individual. Just sit in study hall or in the cafeteria and look at the faces. Many of these faces already show what they will be ten years from now. Choose a physical feature to portray the emotional life of the subject. Be sure to anchor both the present and the future to something as tangible as dishwater, which also serves as a symbol. If you can manage it, include a **zeugma,** as Phillips did, in comparing Maryuma's "large eyes" and "larger hopes." ☼

- - - **Zeugma** is a figure of speech that compares a concrete object and an abstract quality. A single verb serves both:
    Example: She was out of money and out of hope.

PERSONIFYING EMOTIONS: "Stubborn Kisses" by Tess Gallagher

In 1992 Tess Gallagher brought out two books, *Moon Crossing Bridge* and *Portable Kisses*. Many of the poems in *Moon* were reminiscent of her husband, the late Raymond Carver. They are poignant and lovely, and deeply moving to those of us who shared her grief at his too-early death in 1988. *Portable Kisses,* recently expanded and rereleased, contains poems certainly written for Carver, but it also offers poems written for other occasions. As Gallagher writes in the introduction, "There are as many nuances and inflections for kisses as there are lips to kiss and moments in which to bestow them."

Gallagher's trick of studying the kiss rather than the abstract emotional quality of the love that elicited it may become a clever model for new poets. Tess Gallagher knows that the more ethereal the emotion, the more important it becomes to clothe it in concrete terms. She is well aware that human beings live through the senses.

Stubborn Kisses

This kiss won't ride in a car
even with you
in the back seat looking dangerous
as mink. It insists
on running alongside the window
like a piece of the scenery
that won't give you up.

See that splatter, right
where you thought for a moment
it was beautiful? Insects
die over and over
just to prove the sky
is lived-in like this heart
for which I have been given
an inferior sign.

Soon you'll get tired, worrying
about the car running over
my feet, worrying
for the child in me
that's attracting

all these mothers
like a bad parade. You'll
tell the driver to stop
and let you out.

I'll let you
out. I'll stop
and let you out.

You may spot more than one instance in this poem where it seems that Gallagher shows Carver's memory as part of her, both in her own eyes and others'. Is that why she personifies the kiss as running beside the car rather than riding inside with her? Is the kiss intimidated by Carver's shadow? In any case, the element here that makes the poem memorable is the personification of the kiss—running alongside, innocuous as the passing scenery.

☼ FIRESTARTERS

In your own life you may have known many kisses. In a poem, or a series of poems, try Tess Gallagher's idea of personifying kisses. Choose from the list below or substitute your own adjective. In either case, dedicate the poem to Tess Gallagher.

shy	eager
bold	stolen
dutiful	belated
first	last
hesitant	playful
greeting	good-bye
reluctant	obligatory
desperate	guilty ☼

FROM CHARACTER TO CONCRETE OBJECT: A Poem by Lucille Clifton

In "Miss Rosie," Lucille Clifton uses vivid imagery to create more than just a picture with words. She even uses smell:

Miss Rosie

When I watch you
wrapped up like garbage
sitting, surrounded by the smell
of too old potato peels
or
when I watch you
in your old man's shoes
with the little toe cut out
sitting, waiting for your mind
like next week's groceries
I say
when I watch you
you wet brown bag of a woman
who used to be the best looking gal in Georgia
I stand up
through your destruction
I stand up

Notice the carefully chosen details that consistently *show* rather than *tell*. (For example, when we *see* that Miss Rosie wears "Old man's shoes with the little toe cut out," we don't want to be *told* that Miss Rosie is poor or that her feet hurt!) The images all trace themselves back to a central tension: the comparison of Miss Rosie to a sack of garbage, a metaphor society too often associates with old people. However, the marvelous thing here is that Clifton uses that image effectively to convey an opposite theme: Miss Rosie endures! The "best looking gal in Georgia" may have dwindled to a "wet brown bag of a woman," but she goes on. Note how Clifton uses strong repetition to imply her admiration for Miss Rosie's durability: "I stand up, I stand up."

☀ FIRESTARTERS

Using your poet's eye, plan a poem about someone you know casually, or even a complete stranger. Follow Clifton's lead in connecting the person to a tangible object; in this case a sack of garbage. You may choose an object that actually symbolizes the person, or you might be ironic—like Clifton—in using the object only to represent the stereotypical views of others. Construct a list of images in which you connect the subject of the poem to the concrete object. Use this network of images to build your word portrait, but don't forget that imagery calls on senses beyond sight alone: touch, taste, smell, sound. Finally, use skillful repetition to imply—not state—your attitude toward the subject. This poem may be a particularly good spot for line breaks that create double meanings. Note how each of Clifton's lines stands alone, then joins with the next line to add an expanded meaning. The vivid images and the carefully executed line breaks give this poem its substance.

Here are some suggestions of persons you may notice regularly but would not necessarily know well:

a cafeteria worker	a clerk
a bus drive	an usher
an elderly neighbor	a taxi driver
a bag lady	a receptionist
a student in your class	a student on the bus
a policeman	a girl/boy who sits alone at lunch
someone in your church	a teacher

If you think about these people, you may find that some have a bit of history or romance attached to them. Miss Rosie had been "the best looking gal in Georgia." If I were to write a poem about my high school French and Spanish teacher, I would remember the rumors that her husband and infant son had died during an epidemic in Mexico when she was still in her mid-twenties. I would also include the Phi Beta Kappa key she always wore pinned to her lapel; that would give me something tangible to work with. Then I would draw a portrait of an elderly woman with tightly pincurled hair, heavily powdered face, and the same flowered dress day after day. I would smell the cloud of talcum powder as she walked up and down the aisles, drilling us. I would hear her stringy soprano and the pounding of the piano as she led us in singing her translations of "popular" songs dated at least twenty years. I might even taste the sticky glazed donuts she provided each month for our French Club meeting. And certainly I would remember her rolling eyes and nodding head as she indicated exaggerated sympathy for "le pauvre Sept d'Un Coup" in a folktale we translated at length. The list grows and grows. Soon I would have more than enough images to begin a poem, but I would remind myself that I must return in the end to that Phi Beta Kappa key and the dead family. Like Miss Rosie, my teacher was a valiant woman in her own way: she devoted forty years to the public schools; and when they forced her to retire, she taught until her death at a private college. Were all those thousands of students in any way a compensation for her own dead child? I doubt it, but it makes a poignant story.

Look for a hint of mystery or history in the character you choose. Then select the right concrete object to represent it, and you'll be headed toward a poem.   ❁

A POEM OF CONTRADICTION BY ADRIENNE RICH

In "Song," Adrienne Rich invokes a different image in each stanza, showing four facets of "loneliness":

Song

You're wondering if I'm lonely:
OK then, yes, I'm lonely
as a plane rides lonely and level
on its radio beam, aiming
across the Rockies
for the blue-strung aisles
of an airfield on the ocean

You want to ask, am I lonely?
Well, of course, lonely
as a woman driving across country
day after day, leaving behind
mile after mile
little towns she might have stopped
and lived and died in, lonely

If I'm lonely
it must be the loneliness
of waking first, of breathing
dawn's first cold breath on the city
of being the one awake
in a house wrapped in sleep

If I'm lonely
it's with the rowboat ice-fast on the shore
in the last red light of the year
that knows what it is, that knows it's neither
ice nor mud nor winter light
but wood, with a gift for burning

Rich touches on the need for solitude and self-reliance and their intrinsic rewards, then concludes with the image of a rowboat abandoned on

the beach—made of wood, with a gift for burning. How do the images
in this poem fit Rich's role as a poet? Your own role as a writer? How
does this series of vivid contradictions make a positive statement?

✵ FIRESTARTERS

Write your own poem based on a question followed by a contradictory answers. You will seem to agree with the preconception of the question but veer away in an opposite direction as you answer. Repeat the
original assertion three or four times, giving answers through different
images in each stanza. Do not answer the question directly, even in the
last stanza. Imply your answer by searing a memorable image into
your reader's mind through a closure that expands in metaphorical
importance.   ✵

For example, Carrie LeGeune twisted the meaning of "happy" into
a converse application:

Happy

You think I'm happy:
Well, then yes, I'm happy
like the clouds on a stormy day
dragging through their course,
refusing to let the sun melt through.

You assume that I am happy?
All right, I'm happy
roaming in and out of
empty alleys
like silhouettes in the night
absorbing into buildings.
If I'm happy
it must be the joy of living
without destination
never knowing where I fit
like the mallards in winter
flying from icy lake to ice.
            Dedicated to Adrienne Rich

Dean Ramos used this assignment to depict the confusion and search
for identity experienced by anyone who has lived past the age of twelve:

Confusion

You're wondering if I'm confused:
OK then, yes, I'm confused
as a seven-year-old running
frantically in every direction, searching
for his mother,
tears running down his cheeks
in a noisy, crowded mall.
Again you ask if I'm confused,
well, of course, confused
as an abandoned puppy, wondering
where his master has gone, waiting
for the boy who comes home from school
each afternoon
to hug and play with him,
to make him feel safe.

If I'm confused
it must be like the first day at a new school
not knowing who to talk to
or who will answer,
or who will replace the friends I lost.

If I'm confused
it's not with the ability to read,
or write my own name, noticing
a library I'd feel so awkward and lost in,
but knowing that someone inside could help.
        Dedicated to Adrienne Rich

Since Carrie and Dean adhered so closely to Rich's concept and structure, it is only fair that they acknowledge their debt. If they were to use their poems elsewhere, they would need to add a statement such as "Based upon 'Song' by Adrienne Rich."

In the following poem, Sheryl Sullivan took more latitude in responding to the assignment, which is actually the goal. Writing from models teaches new writers how a poem moves, but the ultimate aim is always for them to conceive their own ideas. As you work through this section, look for opportunities to modify assignments to fit your own ideas and your own experience.

Pain

Your eyes question me,
looking for pain scraped in my face
like combing for lice
through a child's hair.

Your face crumbles, reflecting
what my eyes should tell,
like you stumbling in the dark
glancing in a mirror, searching but I'm not there.

I'm hurting you think, covered by a smile
like a mother with a slipped disk, bending
to steady the bicycle for her son
too big for training wheels.

You question too much;
my pain is not from your actions.
It's like a father holding himself steady, accusing
a son of the dent in his car
when he can't remember the night before.

A LESSON IN METAPHORS BY PHILLIP BOOTH

Poets are not intentionally obscure. They don't write poems with "hidden" meanings so that teachers can ask, "What is this poem *really* about?" However, they instinctively write metaphorically since they know, more than anyone, that nothing of significance can be discussed through abstractions. Life is lived through the senses; therefore poets must constantly use imagery to convert abstract ideas into concrete experience. Metaphors are an ideal tool for poets because they allow a story to unfold at two levels: literal and figurative. The literal level clarifies the sequence of concrete ideas and allows for a natural bridge to the symbolic level. Caution: all details must be *literally* true as well as *figuratively* true. The metaphor draws the reader into the real life experience and, in doing so, *implies* the deeper meaning, allowing the reader to feel the twin delights of discovery and surprise.

In "First Lesson," by Phillip Booth, a father is teaching his daughter to float, the first step in learning to swim. His advice is honest and vivid, and it brings back memories to every child who learned to swim in this way. For others, the images are so clear that we seem to relive this experience anyway. By the end of the poem, the reader understands intuitively that more than swimming is being discussed here; this father is in fact giving his daughter a first lesson about life—"lie back and the sea will hold you." Now read "First Lesson," applying the literal experience in each line to the figurative message at the heart of the poem:

First Lesson

Lie back, daughter, let your head
be tipped back in the cup of my hand.
Gently, and I will hold you. Spread
your arms wide, lie out on the stream
and look high at the gulls. A dead-
man's-float is face down. You will dive
and swim soon enough where this tidewater
ebbs to the sea. Daughter, believe
me, when you tire on the long thrash
to your island, lie up, and survive.
As you float now, where I held you
and let go, remember when fear
cramps your heart what I told you:
lie gently and wide to the light-year
stars, lie back, and the sea will hold you.

Sheryl Sullivan competes in both cross country and track, so she drew on her own experience to write "Running," a lesson that works on two levels:

Running

As you run, remember
to watch
the back of the girl
in front of you. Trying
to pass her gives you the strength
to keep going.
There is always a finish
to everything you try for,
and winning here is not important.
The girl you never passed

crosses first and tires.
You finish too, tired
right behind her. You stop
beside her to breathe,
to have her lean on your shoulder.

☼ FIRESTARTERS

Choose a single, self-contained lesson of any kind that you can adapt in this way. On the surface, the speaker will be teaching a skill; underneath, he or she will be teaching an approach to life. Since your poem will be compact and informal, you will need to pay close attention to line breaks. End each line with a strong word that pulls the reader into the next line.   ☼

PERSONIFYING AN OBJECT: "Mirror" by Sylvia Plath

The speaker in the following poem by Sylvia Plath is an inanimate object, a mirror, that literally reflects its owner. Ironically, in the second stanza, the mirror reveals its ability to see into the woman who uses it. In its omniscience, the mirror becomes a lake who drowns the young girl and raises the specter of "a terrible fish," the ugly old woman who is already beginning to replace the girl.

Mirror

I am silver and exact. I have no preconceptions.
Whatever I see I swallow immediately
Just as it is, unmisted by love or dislike.
I am not cruel, only truthful—
The eye of a little god, four-cornered.
Most of the time I meditate on the opposite wall.
It is pink, with speckles. I have looked at it so long
I think it is a part of my heart. But it flickers.
Faces and darkness separate us over and over.

Now I am a lake. A woman bends over me,
Searching my reaches for what she really is.
Then she turns to those liars, the candles or the moon.
I see her back, and reflect it faithfully.

She rewards me with tears and an agitation of hands.
I am important to her. She comes and goes.
Each morning it is her face that replaces the darkness.
In me she has drowned a young girl, and in me an old woman
Rises toward her day after day, like a terrible fish.

☼ FIRESTARTERS

Write a poem in two stanzas following Plath's model. In the first stanza personify an inanimate object closely associated with a person. The first stanza will be a generally straightforward presentation of the object's role in everyday life. The second stanza will be more revealing. Here the object may extend itself into a related metaphor—like the lake—that probes more deeply into the person's fears and feelings. The last line should end with an image that implies the person's future.

You might start by brainstorming with a list of common objects, considering what each object might know about the interior workings of its owner. Here is a list to get you started. As an alternative, you might compile a class list of suggestions: sit in a workshop circle and simply go around the circle with each person contributing an object.

pen	car
key	phone
clock or watch	knife
house	church
boat	glass
computer	television
camera	plate
photograph	trunk ☼

Laura Schock adapted this assignment into a sizzling poem:

She Is a Wine Glass

She is a wine glass,
a fragile ornament
holding the poisonous ambrosia
which rots my tongue

She could spill
venom on linen
slithering towards the already infected

She could shatter
splashing chilled acid
its mission to maim already accomplished

She could stand
hold herself venus still
expecting someone to touch her curves,
bring smoothness to their lips

She waits for me to swallow the first sip

A MEMORY POEM BY LI-YOUNG LEE

Often, in the middle of a familiar action, we are reminded of something
or someone from the past. Often, that person is a parent. In "The Gift,"
Li-Young Lee recreates both the wonder and the fine balance of fear and
tenderness he felt for his father. Even the title of the poem is *wonder*
plus *ful*: full of wonder. Whoever would think of a sliver as a gift? This
gesture of giving and receiving symbolizes the delicate bond between
father and son. Many years later, as Lee removes a splinter from his
wife's thumb, he is engulfed by memory:

The Gift

To pull the metal splinter from my palm
my father recited a story in a low voice.
I watched his lovely face and not the blade.
Before the story ended, he'd removed
the iron sliver I thought I'd die from.

I can't remember the tale,
but hear his voice still, a well
of dark water, a prayer.
And I recall his hands,
two measures of tenderness
he laid against my face,
the flames of discipline
he raised above my head.

Had you entered that afternoon
you would have thought you saw a man
planting something in a boy's palm,
a silver tear, a tiny flame.

Had you followed that boy
you would have arrived here,
where I bend over my wife's right hand.

Look how I shave her thumbnail down
so carefully she feels no pain.
Watch as I lift the splinter out.
I was seven when my father
took my hand like this,
and I did not hold that shard
between my fingers and think,
Metal that will bury me,
christen it Little Assassin,
Ore Going Deep for My Heart.
And I did not lift up my wound and cry,
Death visited here!
I did what a child does
when he's given something to keep.
I kissed my father.

In *Rose,* his first collection of poems, Chicago poet Li-Young Lee comes to terms with the ghost of his father's presence in his life. Even— or especially—after his father's death, Lee finds himself often thinking in terms of his father. Despite the fear his father often provoked, and the harshness of his upbringing, Lee portrays the complex tenderness tinged with awe that he still feels today when a simple action of daily living resurrects an old memory.

✸ FIRESTARTERS

Try using Li-Young Lee's model for a memory poem of your own. Think of someone whom you loved very much: a parent, grandparent, aunt, uncle, teacher, neighbor, brother, sister, and so on. Recreate in your mind, and perhaps a freewriting, a ritual that brings that memory into focus. Use the images to begin a free verse poem. Like Lee, you may wish to insert the trigger of the present into the memory of the past, or you may wish focus solely on memory.

Here are some situations you might consider:

dressing for church	learning to bat
a haircut	first day of school
family vacation	family reunion
filming home movies	birthday party

bar or bat mitzvah
braiding or combing hair
learning to ride a bike
bathing the family dog
hanging up wash
tucking child into bed
rolling down a hill
fishing

first communion
opening Christmas gifts
applying a bandage
repairing or washing the car
baking bread or cookies
reading to a child
burying a bird or goldfish
planting a garden

LEARNING FROM LUCIEN STRYK

"Use either an excellent modifier or none at all."

Lucien Stryk

Lucien Stryk is one of the prime translators of Japanese poetry, and his many years of study are apparent in his own work. Following his own advice to students, Stryk is "chaste with modifiers." His sparing use of adjectives and adverbs results in strong nouns and verbs and a powerful momentum in his lines. Like a Japanese painting, his poems are spare and precise; as in the painting, each brushstroke counts. Stryk often uses terse Japanese verse forms as the building blocks of longer poems. Therefore, his poems show remarkable symmetry both on the page and in their content. As in Japanese art, restraint and balance are everything.

Read "Cherries" and study its imagery, word choice, and construction. Note how the tercets interlock. Each stanza stands on its own, but it also flows into the next, building in a double richness of meaning and metaphor. As in Japanese painting, tones and hues are repeated strongly, and every word works in harmony with the others. Here, Stryk reflects Zen compassion for others and the connectedness of the artist to the world as he moves from eating cherries to "a girl gone bad under the elevator tracks" to "twelve nations bleed(ing)." There is nothing cheap, splashy, or ostentatious here, but each image pulls the reader along relentlessly to a powerful closure.

Try your hand at adapting Stryk's style. Write a poem in tercets, precise in syllable counts and rich in imagery. However, *you may not use more than five modifiers* in the entire poem. Base the poem on a personal action, one in which you, the poet, find metaphorical significance. Use this simple action as the focal point of your poem, with each stanza expanding its metaphorical aspect. The last line should stand alone and epitomize the imagery that leads to it.

An alternative choice is to read "Christ of Pershing Square." Here, a chance encounter with a stranger gives Stryk a powerful metaphorical insight. In this poem your structure will be similar to "Cherries," but the poem will relate an experience rather than focus on an action. Other than that, the restrictions are the same. Every word, every image must relate to one central tension culminated in the closure, which in this case clinches a four-line stanza:

Cherries

Because I sit eating cherries
which I did not pick
a girl goes bad under

the elevator tracks, will
never be whole again.
Because I want the full bag,

grasping, twenty-five children
cry for food. Gorging,
I've none to offer. I want

to care, I mean to, but not
yet, a dozen cherries
rattling at the bottom of my bag.

One by one I lift them to
my mouth, slowly break
their skin—twelve nations

bleed. Because I love, because
I need cherries, I
cannot help them. My happiness,

bought cheap, must last forever.

Christ of Pershing Square

"I can prove it!" the madman cried
And clutched my wrist. "Feel where the nails
Went in! By God, I bear them still!"

Half amused, I shrugged and let him
Press the hand against his suture:
"All right," I said, "they cut you up."

Suddenly those fingers grasped
A hammer, it was I had hoisted
The cross his flung arms formed there.

"Yet," I whispered, "there remains
The final proof—forgiveness."
He spat into my face and fled.

This happened in Los Angeles
Six months ago, I see him still,
White blood streaming, risen from
Cancerous sheets to walk a Kingdom.

Laura Schock wrote "Braid" with a precision learned from Lucien
Stryk. The sparseness of modifiers makes the nouns and verbs reverber-
ate. The few modifiers Laura chooses are perfectly placed. She is following Stryk's advice to "use an excellent modifier or none at all." The
careful line breaks add another dimension of meaning to the poem. Try
reading each line separately, then with the line following it. What do
you discover?

Braid

She made my braids
precise weaving of three even strands
entwined together

Now daddy stands above me
ribbons, brushes, and rubber bands
lined up on the windowsill

Fingers unfamiliar with touching me
tangle my hair, trying to twist
two handfuls into one

Christ he whispers
it doesn't seem so impossible
watching someone else

I grip the edge of the toilet seat
until we decide his braid
off-center and bumpy

was made by an expert.

Jutta Hollis wrote "Safety" after studying Lucien Stryk. Exceeding
the restrictions of the assignment, *she uses only two modifiers*. Realizing
that adjectives and adverbs would only dull the impact of this poem, she
keeps her words as sharp as the speaker's nerves in the last stanza.
Again, note the line breaks and the interlocking stanzas, and consider
how they add a cold undercurrent to the poem:

Safety

wind cuts through me
like my father's voice
through the blanket

cocooned around me,
shutting out
the sound of

mother's cries,
her voice wailing
through bedroom walls, past

pillows pressed to ears.
a child hiding in a corner
waiting for

the sound of chairs scraping
at my nerves
shattering with the slamming door

Jeff Feucht did everything right in applying the Stryk model to a poem about his grandfather. He already had written some early drafts of this idea, but the images were so jarring and rapid that the poem was hard to follow. By dividing the long piece into tercets, each image hits hard, then blends naturally into the next. The effect is much like the Van Gogh self-portrait that inspired this poem: bold, disturbing, and forthright. No dainty adjectives muffle the sounds here, and no flabby adverbs hide the implications. As in "Cherries," Jeff concentrates on one central set of images that unifies the poem:

Those Eyes

Vincent Van Gogh
stole my grandfather's eyes
for a higher cause

they now burn with definition
such clarity shoves aside
his haze

flames
that no element can slow
those eyes leave no debate

blinding intensity
and firehose accuracy
that will never quench

those flames
of vision
and frustration

he has that fire
and God damn i should not
be here

his work is too hot
to touch
its inferno hypnotizes

flames caressing
images
an immutable trance
and no one
can say
i don't care to see

passion like his
so rarely focused,
confusion recedes
where red hair grows

☀ FIRESTARTERS

For this assignment you may begin an entirely new poem or radically revise an early draft of a poem from your portfolio. The principle here is simple: restrict yourself to *no more than five modifiers*. You will find yourself considering each word more closely and selecting stronger, more precise nouns and verbs because of this voluntary restriction. Soon this talent will become second nature when you revise. A good writer is always looking for what can be sharpened or removed. ☀

GOTHIC POETRY BASED ON FRANK STANFORD

> *"Intensity, whether it be in music, dance, business, sports, is the one common thread in anybody I've ever met who is the best at what they do. Some people are outwardly intense and some are inwardly intense, but the important factor is that there is an intensity, a constant intensity. I don't know if you're born with it or if you develop it. I've had it since I was a baby"*
>
> *Billie Jean King*

"A good poem shouldn't be entirely explainable."

Tess Gallagher

Between 1972 and his death in 1978 at the age of twenty-nine, Frank Stanford wrote nine volumes of poetry, all published by small presses and all currently out of print. In 1991, the University of Arkansas, where he had studied both as an undergraduate and as a graduate student, published *The Light the Dead See: The Selected Poems of Frank Stanford*. It is a unique collection with an unforgettable voice. Stanford's southern origins and gothic stories from his childhood run throughout the poems. His voice is terse, vehement, and direct. Although generally narrative in content, the poems shoot out lines as fast and straight as rifle fire. Unlike the more complex patterns of many modern poets, Stanford relies on the unadorned urgency of simple language loaded with metaphor. Read "Freedom, Revolt, and Love"; study its movement and sentence patterns, then write your own gothic narrative based on Stanford's style. Each thought should begin with a subject-verb combination. Many lines will be end-stopped, simple sentences; others may carry an idea over to a second line. However, all lines should begin with capitalized words in order to maintain the directness of tone.

For a gentler approach, read "Memory Is Like a Shotgun Kicking You Near the Heart." This poem also is narrative, rich in image and implication. Base your own poem on an actual or mental retracing of a childhood path that leads to adult discovery. Show the literal path clearly through sharp but terse images, with each stanza presenting a stage along the path. Each stanza should close with an end-stopped line. The last stanza will show your metaphorical arrival at an insight.

Freedom, Revolt, and Love

They caught them.
They were sitting at a table in the kitchen.
It was early.
They had on bathrobes.
They were drinking coffee and smiling.
She had one of his cigarillos in her fingers.
She had her legs tucked up under her in the chair.
They saw them through the window.
She thought of them stepping out of a bath
And him wrapping cloth around her.
He thought of her waking up in a small white building,
He thought of stones settling into the ground.

Then they were gone.
Then they came in through the back.
Her cat ran out.
The house was near the road.
She didn't like the cat going out.
They stayed at the table.
The others were out of breath.
The man and the women reached across the table.
They were afraid, they smiled.
The others poured themselves the last of the coffee
Burning their tongues.
The man and the woman looked at them.
They didn't say anything.
The man and the woman moved closer to each other,
The round table between them.
The stove was still on and burned the empty pot.
She started to get up.
One of them shot her.
She leaned over the table like a schoolgirl doing her lessons.
She thought about being beside him, being asleep.
They took her long gray socks
Put them over the barrel of a rifle
And shot him.
He went back in his chair, holding himself.
She told him hers didn't hurt much,
Like in the fall when everything you touch
Makes a spark.
He thought about her getting up in the dark
Wrapping a quilt around herself
And standing in the doorway.
She asked the men if they shot them again
Not to hurt their faces.
One of them lit him one of his cigarettes.
He thought what it would be like
Being children together.
He was dead before he finished it.
She asked them could she take it out of his mouth.
So it wouldn't burn his lips.
She reached over and touched his hair.
She thought about him walking through the dark singing.
She died on the table like that,
Smoke coming out of his mouth.

Memory Is Like a Shotgun Kicking You Near the Heart

I get up, walk around the weeds
By the side of the road with a flashlight
Looking for the run-over cat
I hear crying.

I think of the hair growing on the dead,
Any motion without sound,
The stars, the seed ticks
Already past my knees,
The moon beating its dark bush.

I take the deer path
Down the side of the hill to the lake,
Wade the cold water.
My light draws the minnows,
Shines through them, goes dead.

Following the shore
I choose the long way home
Past the government camping grounds,
And see where the weeds have been
Beaten down,
Hear the generator on the Winnebago purring.

The children of the tourists
Are under the wheels
Like a covered wagon.
They scratch in their sleep
Until they bleed.

When I get home
I drink a glass of milk in the dark.
She gets up, comes into the room naked
With her split pillow,
Says what's wrong,
I say an eyelash.

The following high school students both wrote from these models.
Charles Noback had already read *The Light the Dead See,* and it
changed his perspective on poetry. He had written two or three drafts of
a tribute poem when I gave him this assignment. Charles found that the
declarative sentences so closely associated with the Stanford style were
perfect for what he wanted to do. The result was an award-winning

poem, "Resting on Sunday." Along with the structure indicated by the assignment, Charles filled his poem with images and allusions associated with Stanford:

Resting on Sunday

It was Sunday morning, your family wasn't home.
You thought they'd gone to church.
Cars were in the driveway.
An old man stood next to a Black Model T
Ford and stared straight at you, waved.
You blinked, rubbed your eyes,
"What the Hell?" you gasped, and looked again.
He was still there, waving, a crooked grin
Ran across the face teeth were missing in,
His smile like boards rotting away in a picket fence.
He was all slow-motion, fighting to get air in his lungs;
His face never flinched, just his chest, heaving up and down.
You tripped over the stairs and broke down your door.
Outside you were slow-motion, sound a vacuum,
The old man's smile, construction paper pasted on his face.
He streaked across your lawn,
Clamped your arms in his bony
Hands and threw you in his polished Model T.
No one saw you, the neighbors were dead.
The car chugged down the asphalt road.
You sat in the back, the old man looked in
His rear view mirror; his reflection nodded and smiled at you.
The seat started to melt, the car sank into the asphalt.
Your screams were absorbed by the black
Car. A puddle of tar was left as the only reminder,
And no one knew you were gone.

You drove on clay roads in the land of Born with Six Toes.
You passed a midget and a man playing a chainsaw.
The old man looked at you and started talking backwards.
You understood. He said, Beware of the moon throwing
   knives.
You awoke on a raft, floating down
A river thick and slow as oil.
It was dark and the moon spotlighted
You on the raft of logs.
You rolled into the river. It swallowed you as a rock sinks in
   tar.

The moon couldn't see you coming
Up for air by the reeds.
The water blurped and formed rings around
You grabbed hold of the Indian
Grass and waded through
Your mirror. Asps tried to follow.
Their fangs broke against glass.
You climbed up the sheer face of your floor
Into your bed as the last pile of
Dirt is thrown on the ground above you.
Cold stone marks where you sleep.

Sheryl Sullivan took the other option. She combined a literal and a metaphorical journey from innocence to knowledge. The path to insight follows the route to a childhood frog pond where two children discover something more troubling than frogs. Sheryl realized that the stanzas outlined in the assignment wouldn't work for her idea, so she wrote her poem in one strong stanza, proving an important point—writing from a model should never be mistaken for writing from a straitjacket:

Tadpoles

We walk next to the woods
On a trail that leads to the fields.
Tom walks in one tire rut
And carries a five gallon bucket.
I walk in the other
And use a fishing net for a walking stick.
I step into the middle of the trail,
A sticker bush reaches for my legs.
We have been walking a long time.
I want to run to where the tadpoles swim.
Tom stops and looks at me.
I hear it too.
We squat to see through the bush.
I kneel beside him.
I see a blanket spread in the field
The boy is on top of the girl.
I know the boy,
He used to ride my bus.
He is my brother's age.
I look at Tom.
He still stares.

I whisper, "Let's go."
He has forgotten I'm here.
He crouches as if he's
In our cardboard house
Under the tops of the bushes.
He starts to run and I follow.
There is a turn in the trail.
We stop.
Through the weeds I see water
Where the tadpoles swam last year.

Wanchay Chanthadouangsy wrote "Frank Stanford and Me" as a response to both Charles Noback and Frank Stanford. Try adapting her trick of pulling images and references from someone else's poem—either a friend's or another author's—and write a poem that echoes or answers the original.

Frank Stanford and Me

I'm drinking coffee
when Frank Stanford walks in.
He has a fishing rod under his left arm,
a box of steak knives in his right hand,
and a crooked smile on his face.
He says to me,
"I'm delirious, fifteen hours
riding a bleeding hog is hell,
I'm thirsty."
I offer him coffee,
he doesn't want any
unless it's the International Foods kind,
French Vanilla to be exact.
He's lucky it is.
I tell him to sit down,
put his things under the table,
I'll get him a cup.
He throws his gear and knives underneath,
plops into one of my wicker chairs,
his gray socks slouch.
He begins to bleed on my chair,
I remind myself to clean it up later.
I pour hot water into a mug,
set it in front of him,

warn him to stir it soon
before the instant powder clumps.
He grabs it with both hands,
takes a sip, then another.
Just like in the commercials, he says,
"This coffee reminds me of a place I know."
He begins his tale:
    "There is a land
    where everyone is born
    with six toes.
    In this land,
    you have to be careful,
    knives are flying all over.
    You wouldn't want one less toe.
    And guess who throws
    these knives—you got it—the moon.
    I'm his sole supplier;
    steak knives, butter knives, Ginsus
    —I have them all.
    And after I make my pitch
    I go fishing in the dark.
    It doesn't matter what I catch,
    I always take something home."
He gets up, pulls up his gray socks,
and says, "I have to go.
My midget is waiting
outside in the Black Model T.
We have to pick up some kid on Sunday."
I thank him.
He walks to the door.
Before he's out,
I say, "Wait, Mr. Stanford;
you forgot your knives and rod."
He smiles crookedly and says,
"Beware of the moon,
just beware of the moon."

✺ FIRESTARTERS

Are you intrigued by the world of Frank Stanford? Use his own poems
and the models by students to venture into gothic territory yourself. ✺

MISSED OPPORTUNITY: A Poem by Tim Seibles

The Good City

I am weighed down by what I
didn't say to you. I
am like some fat man dragging
the moon on a rope. I could have said,
Woman, no word can hold the letters
your body writes on my soul,
but I didn't, so now people see me coming
and want to get their houses
out of the way, but my stone is
so much wider than America. In fact,
my head is growing another head just
to hold what I almost said that Sunday.

Everyone laughs at my trouble
though my hands tremble
like the eyes of someone ready
to beg. They say it's my fault—
they say I have that crabby bedraggled look
of a man whose life is built of things
almost done. I should have told you
about your eyes, about the bright street
I saw in the left one and the sailfish
schooling the bay of the right.
Maybe you would have taken me home,
taken my pulse, taken me upstairs.

But it's late now, you're
somewhere in San Antonio, tugging
at crabgrass in your garden, probably
singing "Besa Me Mucho"
into the cool head of a tulip
while I've got this moon that
leaves the nation flat as buttered toast
behind me—this moon I tow like some
lame hippopotamus on a leash.
I did say, "Your dress is pretty"
but the words came stiffly
as though each were wearing
patent leather shoes, as if

my hands weren't heavy as God
with aching to touch, as if
my thin heart had been smoked
and stubbed out like a cigarette.

So today I have an extra head
that listens only to my fingers,
that hears clearly the ten nervous basses
when their sudden chorus fills my blood

with this hammering, and soon
I will grow one more for remembering
that transparent door in the air,
the whispered dance of your body
beneath that yellow dress,
your hair, your silver-blue eyes—
the good city whose streets I
would wander watching you and the water
with my soul bowed like a cello.

Lindsay Harmon used this model to write her own poem expressing
regret at holding back healthy anger that would have allowed her to
move on more quickly from a dwindling relationship:

No Apologies

There are so many things I
should have said to you.
An avalanche of words
that would have left you
bruised and battered.
Instead, I swallowed anger
until my stomach ached
and bitterness burned
in my mouth.
The rest I put away
for later—
boxes filling closets
until my house is full
of outgrown retorts
and insults never spoken.

But when could I have
told you?

I waited for you to break
the silence, for apology,
at least for closure.
I was never good at writing endings
always expecting
just one more page.
But you've abandoned that story
for your own fairy tale.
I may not have been Cinderella
but you were no Prince
Charming either.
You probably would have dropped
the glass slipper,
swept the pieces under the rug.

☼ FIRESTARTERS

In a poem of three or more stanzas, write about an occasion where you should have said something important to someone but didn't. You may actually use apostrophe, where you address the absent person, or you may simply write in second person "you." Follow Seibles' example in using figures of speech—simile or metaphor—to create appropriate images to show your emotion. Also, allude to or state directly how the missed opportunity has affected you and the person to whom you are addressing the poem. Or, perhaps the person has not been affected at all; perhaps only you have. This could be a love poem, as in the Seibles model, or you could write to a parent, friend, grandparent, teacher—anyone whose life has touched yours.   ☼

CHAPTER 6

FANNING THE FLAMES:
Revision

> **❝** If one wants less fire it can be dampened by putting a shovel of ash on it. If one desires more blaze, a few small sticks of kindling can be added to the top of the fire. **❞**
>
> Raymond W. Dyer,
> *The Old Farmer's Almanac*

"They shouldn't call it writing; they should call it rewriting."

Raymond Carver

In a recent interview, a reporter asked for the secret of my students' success. The answer was easy: revision. Our class is run as a writers' workshop where students work all semester on several pieces of writing. At any given time, their portfolios are filled with pieces taken through several revisions and ready for publication, pieces in various stages of revision, and new pieces waiting for revision. This is how most poets work. Rather than concentrating on a single poem, they prefer to return again and again to several, for they know that writing is a lengthy process. Raymond Carver used to say that he took many of his poems through a hundred revisions. In our workshop we all agree that if Carver needed to revise, we need to revise also. By revision we mean major overhaul, not the dainty insertion of a semicolon in place of a comma.

Some students may feel that revision will interfere with the spontaneity of the moment, the rush of emotion that produced the first draft. If that is the case, I would say that a journal is a good place to preserve this kind of personal writing. All of us have pieces with special meaning for us that we never intend to share with the world. However, any work that we plan to publish will benefit from the critical ears and eyes of sympathetic writers.

Recently I attended a reading by a well-known poet, one of the finest workshop teachers. Naturally, he spoke of revision. A young woman in the audience declared that she herself never revised because she would lose the feeling of the moment. After several polite exchanges, the poet finally asked, "Young lady, why do you think anyone cares how you felt at the moment?"

If we put our egos aside, we must admit that the poet is correct. Unknown readers have no interest in our personal feelings unless we write well enough to pull them into the experience. That is where revision comes in. In fact, as we work through several drafts of a poem, we often find that the real poem is quite different from what we originally expected and that it would never have revealed itself to us had we been unwilling to revise. Ultimately, we find that as time passes we can look at our own work more objectively, ergo, the writing portfolio.

For an example of how this revision and portfolio plan works, I asked one of my students for a random piece midway through revision. Below you will find a reproduction of her original draft. (A revised draft is an ugly thing!) Following that you will read the draft that she gave to me for comments. The distance she has come is apparent, but neither of us considers the poem finished yet. I will tell her that I greatly admire the unity of the images and the sound of the poem. The lines are balanced in length and weight, and the line breaks are excellent. Parallelism and repetition are used well, and the assonance as well as the alliterative sounds are appropriate. However, I will also say that I would like to see more balance in the length of the stanzas, probably through something concrete going on in the second stanza. Over all, I would like to see a more clearly defined sense of place and speaker. Who are these people to each other? Where, exactly, is this poem set? I have the sense that it is outdoors, but is it a meadow? woods? beach? hill? Wherever it is, concrete details of the setting can add to the mood of the poem.

My student will welcome these comments because she knows that, like all of us, she is fallible. Why? Because she already knows the answers to all of my questions, and for that very reason did not see the need to put them on the page. As we write, each of us plays the poem in our mind: we see the people, hear their words, feel the rain, smell the dampness, taste the fear—all those concrete details that the reader needs in order to live the experience with us. Only through friendly criticism by other writers can we step back far enough from our own words to see the murky spots in the canvas.

When it rains

They say your skin
fades   the moon
~~is as~~ paler than ~~milk~~

and your eyes
 look lost
~~have no sparkle~~

 've
but I ~~have~~ seen you*r beauty*

in that moonlight,

underneath the black sky

you glow like a ghost
   in
~~nearing~~ the darkest hours
              that instant flash of certain death.
before dawn, before ~~your death.~~
always been
It's easy for me ~~to find beauty in everything~~

~~in this world, this place,~~
to find beauty in anything
in you. ~~You shine like the moon~~

~~so light filters into my black eyes~~

~~so gently, I don't blink.~~

When it rains, you shudder

your sorrows onto me.

I bathe in them like the

last rays

of moonlight.

~~Then I hold your hot glowing hand~~
And
~~as~~ we descend,
                glowing
two ghosts ~~living~~

~~beyond the moon.~~   *into the edge of emptiness*

The Death of Your Soul

When it rains,
your skin fades
paler than the moon
and the light
of your eyes
shoots out
into blackness
like a star.
But I've seen
your beauty
in that rain
underneath
the black sky
you glow
like a ghost
in the darkest hours
before dawn,
before that flash
of certain death.
It has always been easy
for me to find beauty

in anything,
even in this place
—the edge of emptiness,
even in you.

When it rains
you shudder
your sorrows
onto me and let
me bathe in them
like they are
the last rays
of moonlight.
In this dark hour,
we descend,
two ghosts glowing
beyond that rain
and beauty that
soaks the moon.

REWINDING: An Example of Serious Revision

> *"Almost everything about this movie feels like a first draft—unfelt, unformed, unfinished. And it's not entirely (——'s) fault. As it so often does, Hollywood has mistaken bright promise for full-fledged talent, rushing in to indulge a young artist's self-indulgences, giving him everything he wants but withholding the one thing he needs most: firm but sympathetic challenges to his assumptions, an insistence on rethinking and rewriting until he knows what he wants to say and how to say it."*

> *Richard Schickel,* Time Magazine

Sarah Palomaki saved several of her eight complete redraftings of "A TV Massacre." Reacting to the violent news of a massacre at a local Brown's Fried Chicken restaurant, Sarah dashed off a poem. After numerous reworkings, her final revision is startlingly sharp and taut, a perfect study in revision. As the word *re* plus *vision* connotes, Sarah was able to "see" the scene again and again, each time with increased edge and clarity.

Here is Sarah's final version. When you have finished reading it, read carefully through some of the drafts to witness the journey she took to get to her poem. The drafts are arranged from most recent to most preliminary:

A TV Massacre

They've been shot
the newscaster says
as pictures of the dead
flash on the screen
victims who won't come home
from work after sweating
blood and tears
in the kitchen heavy with smells
of grease and fried chicken

I mention it at dinner
to have it served back
with the mashed potatoes.
"Not at the table," my mother says,
shakes her head and passes
the carrots.

I lay in bed, remembering
yearbook pictures on TV
of life pinched out
like candle flames
Tonight I know I'll dream of them.
My stomach aches, full of food
and television.

A T.V. Massacre

They've been shot
the newscaster says
put pictures (as I read catchy headlines   ) *as pictures*
on the screen,   *of the dead flash*
victims who won't come home   *on the screen*
from work after sweating
blood and tears
in the kitchen heavy with smells
of grease and fried chicken

I mention it at dinner
to have it served back
with the mashed potatoes.
"Not at the table," my mother says,
shakes her head and passes
the carrots.

I lay in bed, remembering
yearbook pictures on TV
of life pinched out
like candle flames
Tonight I know I'll dream of them.
      aches
My stomach‸full of food
and television.
I dream of blood and grease.

A T.V. Massacre

They've been shot
   [newscaster]   *candle flames—*
the newsman says,   *yearbook pictures*
as catchy headlines flash
on the screen,
victims that won't come home
from work after sweating, blood and tears
in the kitchen heavy with the smell
of grease and fried chicken

At dinner I bring it up
to have it served back
~~with a shake~~ with the mashed potatoes
"Not at the table," my mother says,
pursing her lips.

I lay in bed, remembering
(empty faces) of victims
My stomach aches,
~~from too much dinner~~
~~too full of food and television.~~
I dream of grease and blood.

A T.V. Massacre

These stanzas need to echo each other.

They've been shot   *stronger*
~~a massacre~~ (the newsman says)   *opening*
I feel sorry for families
the children (exploded)   *(we)*

at dinner I bring it up
to have it served back
"Not at the table," my mother shakes
her head   *and passes the food*

I lay in bed, still thinking
my stomach full, tired   *stomach—sick, twisted*
close my eyes
dream of dark places   *Maybe it was something I ate.*

TIGHTENING A PROSY POEM

"Early on, revision is the name of the game. You write through struggle. Art is a process of defining what is necessary."

Tess Gallagher

"Dry seeds in a milkweed pod, tick, tick, tick"

Edgar Lee Masters, "Petit the Poet"

Tick. Tick. Tick. Petit's words made sounds but said nothing. He worked so hard at being literary that he ignored the simple instincts of poetry surrounding him. Poetry, after all, is more than just a form for arranging words on a page; it is *what* the words say and *how* they say it.

Perhaps the most common problem beginning poets face is learning to edit their own work. They are tempted to leave anything they write because they project themselves along with the words onto each page. If they are unfamiliar with workshopping, they may interpret suggestions for revision as a personal attack. But empty words, like empty pods, just make noise, and eventually new poets begin to recognize the problem. The form looks right, but something is wrong with the words. Soon they realize that their poems read like paragraphs; that they set out to write

"Stopping by Woods on a Snowy Evening" and ended up with *National Geographic*. When this happens, poets refer to the work as *prosy*.

The solution, of course, is to develop an ear for the way poetry *sounds*. Unfortunately, this takes time and determined practice. You can aid the development of your own inner ear by reading good poetry, studying what makes it work, and looking at your own work in comparison. How can you sharpen your word choices, pattern your lines more carefully? Learning the basics of metrics can help. By scanning your lines you can pinpoint trouble spots and revise accordingly. You can examine each word choice, especially modifiers. An ample harvest of modifiers usually reveals a weak crop of nouns and verbs. Also, look for unplanned repetition of words or phrases; if it wasn't planned, it shouldn't be there! Padding a poem with words is like wrapping a jumper cable in cotton wool: it's not going to generate electricity.

The following poem was written by a promising high school student at a literary festival where I conducted a workshop in revision. Before we began our work, I held up a fresh kiwi and told the group, "This is your poem before revision." The ugly brown fuzz made my point. Then I peeled and sliced the kiwi to reveal a succulent green fruit with delicate dark seeds. "This is your poem after revision," I said. I then placed the plate on the podium to remind us of our task—paring away the fuzz. Poets call this process *tightening*—removing unnecessary words—and *sharpening*—replacing weak words or phrases with power nouns and verbs.

Empty Doorway

An open doorway,
An empty doorway
To a hall of white walls.
I lay there waiting . . .
        waiting . . .
        waiting . . .
Hopelessly for someone, anyone—
But no one comes.

Today will be like any-other-day . . .
The same sounds,
    same room,
    same silence.

Any change would be welcome,
An unexpected visit, a friend.

Sometimes the shadow of my I.V. machine
Falls from the bed to the wall.
And it is the only thing that moves,
Anywhere at all.

I remember,
It—was—Always Elsewhere . . .

I shut my eyes tight against the
Light from the window,
And only the dull colors remain
In my memory,
The vision never coming into focus.

The hourglass is no longer intrinsic,
The clock moves in only one direction
And never stops at all;
But if it did—Nothing would change.

Each night I count the footsteps in the hall,
And each night I get the same number.
And when the sounds of the steps cease,
I count the silence they leave.

This student has a natural talent for poetry. Her lines generally end with strong words and the breaks are carefully made. With only one exception—*intrinsic*—her words choices are sharp. *Intrinsic* does not fit the simple, straightforward diction of the poem, and it is not concrete. In another poem it might work well, but here it calls attention to itself. There is even a rudimentary sense of movement, or pacing, in this original version. All it required was a general tightening, or elimination of weak repetition, redundancy, and unnecessary words. The first task of a poet who has just drafted a poem is to look over it carefully *to see what can be taken out.* Once the dead wood is removed and tossed into the fire, only live wood remains, and the poem is made stronger by the pruning.

Here is the revision that emerged from the workshop. Note the improvements in conciseness, concreteness, sound, parallelism, rhythm, and line breaks. Also notice the deletion of weak modifying words and phrases and unnecessary conjunctions. Tightening reveals a vigorous poem that had been nearly smothered by unnecessary words. Its immediacy puts the reader into the hospital room, sharing the experience.

Empty Doorway

An empty doorway opens
to a hall of white walls,
all holding me in.
I lie waiting for someone to come.

Today will be like any-other-day,
same sounds
same room
same silence.
Any change would be welcome.

From the bed to the wall,
the shadow of my I.V. falls,
the only thing that moves.
I shut my eyes against the light;
the colors dance
without focus.

The hourglass runs out of sand,
the clock moves on.
Nothing changes.
Each night I count the footsteps in the hall;
each night the count is the same.
I count the silence they leave.

☼ FIRESTARTERS

Look through your portfolio for first drafts of poems. Choose one for revision, and work through it relentlessly, looking for opportunities to cut unnecessary words and sharpen word choices. As Ernest Hemingway said, anything that is obvious shouldn't be there.   ☼

REVISION THROUGH SHARPENING

"I don't fall," the boy said, "because I've got a deep respect for the concrete surface and because when I make a miscalculation, instead of falling, I turn it into a new trick."

Joy Williams

When we begin writing poems, most of us err on the side of excess; we use too many words and not necessarily the right words. We have been told all through school that adjectives are "descriptive," so we use lots of adjectives. We may even fall into a pattern of padding every noun with at least one adjective, often more. As poets we love language, so we may find it difficult to part with a favorite word, even though we suspect that our teacher is right in suggesting revision. This is the point where it becomes essential to step back and try to view our work objectively, and that is the beauty of a workshop. If eight others believe the poem needs sharpening, we have to take that recommendation seriously. Here is an example of what some minor cutting and word changes did for Dan Acton's poem:

Inheritance

Her blistered fingers crawled
like red ants over sheaves
of parchment as brown and soft as mouse's fur
the shuffled leaves
overflowed onto the floor
and piled in a heap around
her feet, hard as horns
encased in humid pink slippers
as thick broken fingernails raked through
receipts, photographs, armadillo swatches of fabric.
cigarette ashes smoldered into the wrinkles between
the papers in the drawer.
she blinked over photos of herself as a grandchild
eyes skipping ahead of her hands
until the envelope appeared.
she touched the edges, it cracked open
dollars the color of spoiled cabbage leaves
her inheritance in advance.

The poem above is the first draft Dan showed us. We were immediately drawn to its strong imagery and implied narrative. Our workshop suggested crossing out some words, mostly modifiers, and changing the verbs to present tense. Here is the revision:

Inheritance

Her blistered fingers ~~crawled~~ *scurry*
like red ants over sheaves
of parchment as brown and soft as mouse's fur

the shuffled leaves
overflow~~ed~~ onto the floor
and pile~~d in a heap~~ around
her feet, hard as horns
encased in ~~humid~~ pink slippers
her   ~~as thick~~ broken fingernails rake~~d~~ through
receipts, photographs, armadillo swatches of fabric.
cigarette ashes smolder~~ed~~ into the wrinkles between
~~the~~ papers in the drawer.

she blink~~ed~~^s over photos of herself as a grandchild
eyes skipping ahead of her hands

until the envelope appear~~ed~~^s.

she touch~~ed~~^s the edges, it crack~~ed~~^s open
Inside,   dollars the color of spoiled cabbage leaves
~~her inheritance in advance.~~

Once he had made those changes, Dan found other opportunities to sharpen the imagery. The final revision received a first-place award in Best Illinois Poetry and Prose:

Inheritance

Her fingers scurry
like red ants over sheaves
of parchment
brown and soft as mouse's fur.
The shuffled leaves overflow onto the floor
and pile around her feet hard as horns
encased in pink slippers.
Her broken fingernails rake through
receipts, photographs, armadillo swatches of fabric,
she blinks over photos of herself as grandchild,
eyes skipping ahead of her hands
until the envelope appears.
She touches the edges, it cracks open;
inside, dollars the color of spoiled cabbage.

☼ FIRESTARTERS

Choose one of your own poems to present to your workshop for suggestions. Consider all suggestions seriously, but remember that the final decision always belongs to you. Assure yourself that every word in your poem is the best word for that spot, that it is necessary, and that it works with every other word in the poem.   ☼

ADDING LAYERS OF MEANING: Literary Allusions

As a junior, Sean Dempsey was working with a poem based on a painting by Edward Hopper when we both saw the potential for his poem to assume sharper meaning through creating a chain of literary allusions. For example, if I were to refer to a "midnight ride" and lantern signals, "one if by land, two if by sea," I could assume that most of my readers would recognize these as allusions to Paul Revere.

Sean had chosen to write about a painting in which a forlorn woman sits alone at a desk in sterile surroundings. She seems to be motionless and frozen in time. Even in the first draft he had instinctively reached for ancient Egyptian imagery. The deletions and additions are Sean's:

> The beauty queen wanted more
> and now you've got it.
> Your ivory white skin,
> silk smooth in Georgia
> cracks in the New York sun.
> Your building, like a pyramid
> holds royalty
> buried with their servants.
> Spirits
> ~~Ghosts~~ scream from the walls
> ~~dark.~~
> ~~Your desk, makeshift~~
> The ceiling lights can't pierce.
> Your desk is false,
> pushed up where a desk shouldn't be,
> ~~You answer phones and open mail~~
> ~~Windows are for l~~

against a window.
Windows are for looking in
    shouldn't
You ~~can't~~ do that in New York.
Its all surface,
your job, you.
You show legs and wear strap~~s~~ *less*
dressing an oasis in the desert.
You're alive, more than the rest.
but your eyes.
Your eyes are dead.

Sean tightened the wording in his second revision. The poem moves more certainly and the images are sharper. He was right to eliminate the two-line editorial comment that had opened the first draft, and he had already injected the clever line break between *strapless* and *dresses*. The editing marks are Sean's:

Your ivory white skin,
silk smooth in Georgia
cracks and yellows in the New York sun.
behind the glass, in the office
~~where you~~
~~Brick~~ Built with pyramid ~~blocks bricks~~
it holds dead royalty
their servants buried live.
Spirits scream from the walls

                                        a
and faceless scarabs scurry into ~~the~~ dark
the ceiling lights can't pierce.

Your desk is false,
pushed where a desk shouldn't be,
against a window.
Windows are for looking in.
You shouldn't do that in New York.
The phone never rings and the letters get shredded.
it's all surface.
Your job, you,
~~wearing~~ showing leg and wearing strapless
dresses an oasis in the desert
You're alive,
like No one else to
but your eyes
your eyes are dead.

This second draft marked a critical point in the development of the poem. Sean showed it to me but said he wanted to revise some lines before he would be ready for specific feedback. I was pleased with the originality of the Egyptian tomb imagery in a poem about a modern New York office, so I simply gave him Shelley's sonnet, "Ozymandias," to read, along with the general comment that it might add depth to his symbolism.

As my students work, I often move quietly around the room offering to look at poems in progress. Sean had taken "Ozymandias" home and finished draft #3 the night before. He was ready for a serious reader. The poem now had a title, "Egypt," which reflected the increasing importance of that second layer of images. Sean had already done some fine-tuning himself: for example, he realized that ivory is always white; thus "ivory white" had been redundant. "Ivory" worked better than "white" with the imagery of Egyptian wealth locked in a tomb. On this draft the editing marks are mine:

Egypt

Your ivory skin,
pure in Georgia
cracks as the New York sun
swallows you, behind ~~the~~ glass.
Outside your office, bricks
of sandstone pyramid blocks stacked
into a tomb, the air inside thick
with must, ~~and~~ decay.
Dead ~~royal~~ businessmen leave   *one or the other*
their legacy,
ruined, shattered faces, trunkless legs.
Each Ozymandias
buries himself with ~~his~~ servants.
In ~~a~~ dark the ceiling lamps can't pierce,
your hair <u>is</u> still sculpted.

The phone
on your desk
never rings and your letters <u>are</u> shredded.
This job,
it's all surface,
and the tourists
buy you
piece by piece
as the natives chip you apart.

You show leg and wear strapless
dresses, a blue mirage in the desert.
You're alive,
[unlike] not like the barren streets and alleys   **> ?**
but your eyes,
your eyes are dead.

In this draft Sean refers directly to "each Ozymandias." He is zeroing in
on the target of this poem. I suggested that he study Shelley's poem
again and choose some striking images—allusions—to insert into his
own work. The next day he offered draft four to a senior, Ridgely Dunn,
for comment. The editing marks are hers:

Egypt

Your ivory skin,
pure in Georgia
cracks as the New York sun
swallows you, behind glass.
Outside your office,
sandstone pyramid blocks stack
into a tomb, air inside thick
with must, decay.
Dead businessmen leave their legacy,
ruins, shattered faces, trunkless legs.
Each Ozymandias
buries himself with servants.
In dark the ceiling lamps can't pierce,
your hair stays sculpted.

The phone
on your desk   *shred your letters*
never rings and you~~r letters are shredded.~~
This job, it's all surface
and the tourists buy you
piece by piece
as the natives chip you apart.
You show leg and wear strapless
dresses, a blue mirage in the desert.
Your body's alive,
unlike the barren streets.
~~But your eyes,~~   *Poem needs to be drawn together.*
~~your eyes are dead.~~

The specific allusions to "Ozymandias" add another layer of imagery to the poem. Since Shelley's sonnet is standard reading in the British literature studied in most American high schools, Sean can assume that most adult readers would recognize the allusions to "shattered face(s)" and "trunkless legs." Now his readers see Shelley's image of the statue of a pharaoh reduced to rubble along with Sean's image of a Georgian beauty mummified in New York.

Sean's next draft shows a sharp sense of closure not present in earlier versions. Shelley's sonnet closes with the vast expanse of sand that outlived the pharaoh's name; Sean's poem closes with a blue mirage in the desert, something that never really existed. In both closures, human memory has been obscured by time. Reading "Ozymandias" helped Sean to see where his poem was longing to go:

Egypt

Your ivory skin,
pure in Georgia,
cracks as the New York sun
swallows you
behind glass.
Outside your office,
sandstone blocks stack
into pyramids, air inside thick
with rot from the dead.
Businessmen leave
their legacy of ruins,
shattered faces, trunkless legs.
Each Ozymandias
buries himself with servants.
In dark the ceiling lamps can't pierce,
your hair stays sculpted
into bleached rows.

The phone
never rings.
You shred your letters.
This job, all surface.
~~the tourists buy you~~
~~piece by piece~~   } *delete*
~~as the natives chip you apart.~~
You show leg and wear strapless
dresses, a blue mirage in the desert.

Sean took this draft to a conference where poet Lucien Stryk worked with a group of advanced high school students. The consensus there was that the poem is doubly vivid due to Sean's twin layers of imagery: everything that applies to Ozymandias also applies to the woman. In fact, the workshop caused Sean to realize that his reference to "tourists" and "natives" was superfluous; it weakened the central tension of the poem. Below is the final revision:

Egypt

Your ivory skin
pure in Georgia
cracks as the New York sun
swallows you
behind glass.

Outside your office,
sandstone blocks stack
into pyramids, air inside thick
with rot.
Businessmen leave
their legacy of ruins,
shattered faces, trunkless legs.

Each Ozymandias buries himself with servants.
In dark the ceiling lamps can't pierce,
your hair stays sculpted
into bleached rows.

The phone never rings.
you shred your letters.
This job, all surface.
You show leg and wear strapless
dresses, a blue mirage in the desert.

✷ FIRESTARTERS

1. Have someone in your workshop read aloud (slowly) the final revision of "Egypt." Do not read along; just listen. Now, have the reader do the same with the first draft. Finally, have the reader go back to the final revision and read it aloud as you read it silently on the page.

Discuss your reaction to the three readings. Which was clearer? Which sounded smoother? What images did you see in your mind as you listened? What words or images lingered in your mind after the poem was finished?

2. Look through your journal and portfolio for a poem to which you can add a layer of literary allusions. If nothing seems right, choose a poem you are interested in revising and take it to your workshop group for suggestions. Since everyone has a different background, individuals can often lend you a fresh approach to your own work. ✺

CHAPTER 7

TENDING THE FIRE:
Poems from Your Own Life

❝Eventually the fore and back logs will burn through; as this happens they should be moved into the center of the fire and replaced with new logs, once more well-bedded in ash.**❞**

Raymond W. Dyer,
The Old Farmer's Almanac

KEEPING THE FIRE BURNING

Tribal societies prized fire and carried it with them whenever they moved. The fire never went out. It fanned and it waned; it jumped from one location to another; but it never escaped the close attention of its guardians. The fires of poetry require the same attention; they will follow you faithfully throughout your life if you give them minimal attention.

First, you must *intend* to keep them burning. At the onset you will need a permanent base for the fire, then, as you grow, it will follow. To keep inspiration smoldering, you will need to live your life as a poet, seeing poetry in the unusual, the commonplace, even the familiar. Once you train your eye and your imagination, you will find poetry to be as easily portable as the tribal fire. It will be your warmth and your companion.

BUILDING A TRIGGERING TOWN

"Our triggering subjects, like our words, come from obsessions we must submit to, whatever the social cost."

Richard Hugo

In 1979, Richard Hugo's lectures and essays on poetry were gathered for publication in *The Triggering Town,* which has subsequently become the bible of university poetry workshops. In the title lecture, Hugo talks about obsession, the need to be obsessed by the subjects one chooses to write about. While he believed that poems come out of the poet's life, he always insisted upon the role of imagination. Hugo believed that our life-long exposure to information-oriented writing can lead us to write poems as if they were essays. His antidote to the "just the facts, ma'am" approach to writing is the creation of an imaginary "triggering town," a secure home base from which the imagination can operate.

As you read, you will find that many poets have consciously or unconsciously taken Hugo's advice. Their poems seem to grow out of a common landscape loosely tied to their own real world. While the poems may be truth in general, they are fictitious in detail. Sometimes the greatest truths are dressed as imagination. You may choose to build your triggering town on the foundations of your own hometown, but you will change the buildings, the inhabitants, the events to suit your own obsessions—those needs that drive you to write.

In 1993, Ruth Forman published her first collection of poetry, *We Are the Young Magicians.* Her work is solidly grounded in a sense of place that allows her imagination to reach out in intriguing and risky directions. The following poem paints a vivid picture of Forman's triggering town:

Young Cornrows
Callin Out the Moon

we don have no backyard
frontyard neither
we got black magic n brownstone steps
when the sun go down

we don have no backyard
no sof grass rainbow kites mushrooms butterflies
we got South Philly summer
when the sun go down

cool after lemonade n black eye peas
full after ham hocks n hot pepper greens
corn bread coolin on the stove
n more to watch than tv

we got double dutch n freeze tag n kickball
so many place to hide n seek n
look who here Punchinella Punchinella
look who here Punchinella inna zoo

we got the ice cream man

we got the corner store
red cream pop
red nails Rick James the Bump the Rock
n we know all the cheers

we got pretty lips
we got callous feet healthy thighs n ashy knees
we got fiine brothas we r fiine sistas
n
we got attitude

Gary Soto draws on his triggering town in *Black Hair*, a collection
of poems drawn from his own life. Jackie, a childhood friend, is one of
the recurring characters:

Brown Girl, Blonde Okie

Jackie and I cross-legged
In the yard, plucking at
Grass, cupping flies
And shattering them against
Each other's faces—

Smiling that it's summer,
No school, and we can
Sleep out under stars
And the blink of jets
Crossing up our lives.
The flies leave, or die,
And we are in the dark,
Still cross-legged,
Talking not dogs or baseball,
But whom will we love,
What brown girl or blonde
Okie to open up to
And say we are sorry
For our faces, the filth
We shake from our hair,
The teeth without direction.
"We're ugly," says Jackie
On one elbow, and stares

Lost between jets
At what this might mean.
In the dark I touch my
Nose, trace my lips, and pinch
My mouth into a dull flower.
Oh God, we're in trouble.

When two friends and I decided to start a literary magazine, we invented a triggering town loosely based on our own hometown. However, Bluff City is smaller, dirtier, and scrappier than Elgin, and its people are mostly imaginary.

When she can't sleep, the mayor of Bluff City runs its street names through her head: Congdon, Summit, Franklin; and fashions new ones, all set in white block letters on deep-green city issue street signs: Pitchdark, Cointoss, Carchase. There's a pair of signs on every corner of Bluff City, making a cross with one another, but no two pairs are ever the same. Her grandfather, who was born here, and worked at the watch factory until he died, her grandfather once told her, "A wish is held where two lines cross. That's why we cross our fingers when we wish." She would like to live on a street named Smackdab, but has told no one. Imagine her at a city council rezoning session, suggesting Grove be changed to Smackdab, insisting on it, growing belligerent as the faces around her stop smiling. It's better she keeps to herself how much she'd enjoy seeing "410 Smackdab Avenue" under her name on envelopes. Otherwise, she thinks, she'd be out of a job, and Bluff City's as bad a place as any to be out of a job smackdab in the middle of your life, looking for work.

☀ FIRESTARTERS

Create a triggering town, based partly on reality, partly on imagination, and start growing your own poems. Who will live in your town? What are their dreams and obsessions? How will they reflect yours? Record the details of your triggering town in your journal, either through a series of freewritings or lists of images. Do as we do with Bluff City; return to your triggering town time after time for ideas.   ☀

FAMILY STORIES

Your best source of poems is your own experience. That doesn't mean you need to resurrect your diary or divulge your best friend's secrets. Just look around you—at your own family, neighbors, friends, even the people at work or at church. Each of them has a story worth telling. The job of the poet is to find it.

Begin your search at home. Plumb your childhood for those moments or memories that need to be preserved in a poem. Talk to your parents and grandparents; call on those stories buried in the corners of their minds. The examples that follow may give you ideas for poems from your own family stories.

When he was seventeen, my father mangled his right index finger in a punch press at his father's box factory. Suddenly, through one stroke of a steel punch, his future was canceled. He lost his scholarship to medical school, and in the end, even lost the finger. However, my father found that he gained something priceless as a result of his loss. (Notice how the lost finger remains the central focus of the poem in all three stanzas.)

Loss

My father lost his finger
to a punch press
when he was seventeen.
A small town GP amputated

his right index finger
and strapped the hand
high on his chest.
For almost a year
pokers of pain burned
through the stump
and my father
chewed aspirin.

Alone with the pain
he must have planned
how to turn a page
lift a cup
whether to point
using that second finger;
the simplest gesture
a matter of design.
He must have considered
how infinitesimal the miscalculation
that cost him a finger,
how narrow the line
between wholeness and loss.

For the rest of his life
my father wore his gloves
with the right index finger
punched in.
He hated anything empty.
Whenever he told the story
he always ended by saying,
"If I hadn't lost my finger
I wouldn't have met your mother."
Then he'd reach for her hand,
squeeze her index finger
between his thumb and second finger,
and his hand was whole.

Michelle Van Ness's mother tells about the months she spent with Michelle's father, a pipeline welder who traveled from job to job and state to state, never earning quite enough money to feed them. Her mother remembers how she would open a can of beans, set it on the radiator to "cook," and serve it as their evening meal. A small but telling object like the can of beans can create the fabric of a poem. The poem begins and ends with that can of beans, a fitting symbol of the life Michelle's mother found herself living:

Old Men and Dirty Pigeons

Yawning, she twists the can open, pulls the lid
away from the steel lip. Her nose wrinkles,
smell of beans and dust permeates the air humid with July
heat, she puts the can on the radiator
snoring on low. Any higher and the heat would fog
the windows like tears that floated
in her eyes, and fell to her cheeks
red from alcohol
and blows from his hands.
She meets him at midnight in Battery Park
next to the wrought iron bench where old
McAfferty fed pigeons when she was five
and found amusement in birds and laughter.
Now she waits, alone, no birds to feed, no old man
to sit next to, only hair on her neck
touching her. Smiling as he approaches
her, lamp light defining the edge of his brow, his jaw;
he whispers a joke to make her smile, takes her arm,
leads her away from the bench to the bar across from the
    park.

After a few hours, maybe three, the beans are warm and stale.
She slides the can from the radiator
to the table, pokes them with her fork, wishes
on clearing skies, old men, and dirty pigeons.

Wanchay Chanthadouangsy looks at the canna bulbs she is planting and remembers her mother's stories of life in Laos before the war in Vietnam changed everything. Wanchay's interlocking stanzas and carefully worded line breaks add another dimension to this poignant poem:

Cannas

I stab a rust-flecked spade
hard into gray earth,
frost crackles morning
near my knees.

Already green shoots
through the plastic
where droplets cling,
though not too late to plant, I know

Mother was young
when cannas peeled
like cones of China silk,
each petal curved like lips
kissed by rain
dried by morning sun
pressed over nails that I imagine
peeled by water buffalo,
plowing solid fields, yoked
like two gallon pails
balanced over dust trails
where rice paddies greened to horizons,
not reaped until the last rains
washed away water marks
or tear stains, I can't tell

Mother's flesh was pink
—a shade of the red she loves
underneath the petals
where cannas bloom late
concealing their colors until fall
of sun, leaves, or snow, so I remember
to plant early.

☼ FIRESTARTERS

Talk to your own family—parents, grandparents, aunts, uncles, cousins—and uncover the many poems that are surely waiting to be written. Choose the story most appealing to you now for this assignment, but record the other stories in your journal to be pulled out on a rainy day.   ☼

POEMS FROM YOUR PAST

Flannery O'Connor once said that anyone who survived a childhood has a lifetime of stories. This is equally true for the poet. If you're looking for a universal experience, here it is. Who hasn't been a child?

Who hasn't skinned a knee, caught a lightning bug, played tag under the street light on a hot summer night? Sometimes these memories are wistful and innocent; sometimes they are portents of the adult struggles ahead.

Jeff Feucht remembers when being six years old presented possibilities as limitless as Superman's—until his cape tangled:

naive

after the grilled cheese
your dad would cut
red plastic capes
from the big roll
in your garage

we wore them tucked under
T-shirts left to flap
against our backs
like an encouraging
flag

we'd jump on our bikes
ride, ride the wind
lifting our capes
to the skies, we flew
at such high altitude on those sidewalks

six year old supermen
undaunted by kryptonite
or attractive reporters
a bicycle
spoke
our lone weakness

cape sure to entangle
we plummet from the stratosphere
and hit our groins
on that damn bar
on our way down

Children of all ages frequently face pressure to conform to unspoken standards of behavior or appearance. Those who do not conform are often the targets of cruel taunts and teasing. Sheryl Sullivan transforms the unkind comments into a moving poem:

Girl Poem

I am not a girl
they say, girls
wear dresses,
pretty dresses,
eat silence,
lips pressing
to forks.
But I have been
with a boy,
I say, holding
his hand.

Tell me,
tell me why
they smirk.
I would blush,
they say, if
I were a girl.
Angry now,
I say I am too,
I like flowers,
I wish on stars.
That, they say,
does not
make me a girl.

I squeeze my fingers
to my temples.
They say, if
my nails were not
bitten
I could be
beautiful.
I try hiding them
between my legs.
My hands,
they say, are
dangerous.
They say try
blushing,
try biting my lips
which only puff and whiten.

They do not
try their smiles,
my bitten fingers
still throb. Girls,
they say, write
silly poems,
cry if they know
their ugliness.
Girls watch
the moon
rise.

Danelle Hlavacek writes of a family blown apart by a tempest of emotion:

A Father's Touch

Mood swings cause tornadoes.
I watch your touch build
a force five hurricane
tears our home apart.
Red rain soaks my clothes.

I struggle to stand as the earthquake ends,
my voice lost in the wind.
I whisper your words
strike electrical lines,
short circuiting communication.
You pluck hair
like leaves
in the deadly aftershock.

Lightning bolts through your eyes
as I ask if I'm Daddy's
little girl.

☼ FIRESTARTERS

Test Flannery O'Connor's theory by examining your own childhood and adolescence for ideas. List your memories, images, and ideas in your journal; then return to them from time to time to make poems.   ☼

BEYOND HALLMARK: Poems That Show You Care

Sometimes you want better than the Hallmark "best." Sometimes you want "I love you" to be more than words, more than a generic greeting-card verse suitable for thousands. You want "I love you" to be individual and original. Your love for another person is not exactly like anyone else's love, and sometimes the need to communicate that emotion is so strong that only a poem written especially for that loved one will do.

Like many young poets, you may worry that your words will sound flowery and trite. You have good cause for concern: most poems about love do sound sappy! Why? Perhaps because it is easy to write a forgettable love poem and difficult to write a memorable one. Our culture is so saturated with clichés about love that they leap into our minds whenever we set out to write.

There are as many kinds of love as there are people, and most of us feel different kinds of love for the people close to us: family members, friends, boyfriend, girlfriend, and others. In order to avoid cloying stereotypes, you need only to look at what makes the person in your poem unique. Luis Hernandez wanted to write a Mother's Day poem for the foster mother who had taken him in and loved him as a son. Even now that he is an adult, she remains a steadying force in his life, holding warmth and love in the same hands that tend the garden and bake bread:

Seven Days

In the calendar
I've made for you
there are no holidays.
No month-ends
or beginnings.
Only seven seamless days.
I work my way through
all of them.

Mornings,
sunlight
through the clouds
finds me:
caught between dull chores
and routine.
I pause to wonder

how much love
I could hold
in my two working hands.

Then think of yours
with the wonderful warmth
of bread and sun-baked soil.
Your fingers
when they touch me,
feel like ten miracles
waiting to happen.

At night,
I have the moon
with its quiet pull
on both the water and me.
And starlight that falls down
all around
filling the moments
until I can see you again—
that brilliant point in time
that requires nothing more
from you and me
than the small gesture
the long laughter
and a strong steady measure of love.

Of course love comes in many guises, and most poets at one time or another feel the need to write a poem about romantic love: love gone right or love gone wrong. None of us considers our love ordinary or banal, so we must be wary of clichés when writing of it. Remember, Hallmark gears its product for mass-market appeal; if your love is unique, write about it in unique terms.

In the following poem, Sarah Haberstich releases her last ties to an unfaithful love and watches them evaporate like smoke:

Therapy

When I remember touching
you, my hands
turn November cold,
shake like dead leaves
clinging to rejecting branches.
You said you met her
in Corpus Christi; exploring.

I said I am a cave
filled with wonders.
What more can she
be? Change, you insisted.
You have planted seeds
of clichés in my mind.
A forest of "just friends"
and "someone elses"
begins to flourish
around me.
I light my cigarette,
inhale, feel smoke burn
my throat, menthol
deceivingly medicinal,
Exhale, watch your spirit
float away on the wind.

☼ FIRESTARTERS

Choose someone in your life who deserves to know he or she is loved. Focus your imagery around a tangible trait like the gardening and the baking of bread in Luis's poem, then link that trait to the emotion. You might also follow Luis's idea of offering a "gift" that fits the love you feel, in his case a calendar with no beginnings or ends. Since calendars are calculated according to stars and the moon, the opening and closing stanzas of this poem create a subtle symmetry. "Sunlight" in the second stanza speaks to "starlight" in the fourth stanza; "mornings" in the second speaks to "night" in the fourth. Everything is tied warmly together with light from the stars, the moon, and "that brilliant point in time" when Luis will see his foster mother again. Make your own poem unique by selecting images that tie themselves to the subject as closely and gently as these.   ☼

REMEMBERING A GRANDPARENT

Grandparents are natural subjects for poems because we tend to remember them with our hearts as well as our brains. We see them through a scrim that softens the edges of reality and colors them with nostalgia. Often we remember them involved in some familiar task or action, just as Tina Pomeroy shows her grandmother "Making Potica." Tina was a senior at Interlochen Arts Academy when she wrote this poem about her Yugoslavian grandmother:

Making Potica

We sit in Gramma's kitchen,
warmed by the oven,
our fingers aching from cracking nuts
for the *potica*.

We watch Gramma
as she takes off her ring,
sets it on the windowsill
next to her birthday fern.
The bread swell of her belly
tucked under an apron,
she rolls up her sleeves,
arms showing round and white
like the dough she begins to knead between her fingers.

Against the table she slaps the dough,
folds it in on itself
again and again.
Flour rises in storms,
clouds around her face
Her body knows the rhythm
of this bread
as the peach trees of Rijeka
know the seasons.

Gramma rolls the dough thin,
ladles out the thick swell
of cellar honey, spreads it smooth.
She sows the nuts like seeds,
sprinkles on the sweet *rayene*
dried from the grapes
whose vines tangle across the back porch.

"*Yez patee
ba gzita Normaraila,*"

she sings and winks at us.
But we don't understand
those words she couldn't leave
in Belgrade.
We only know the song of her dough,
the music she makes with her hands.

Jana Thompson remembers her grandmother in vivid images of an itinerant life that culminate in the strawberry plants that now anchor her existence:

Strawberry Plants

I outgrew my grandmother.
By the time I was ten,
I could see over her head,
She was delighted
to see something change without her.

I never knew her house was small
until I outgrew my grandmother.
Halls dark and narrow,
tiny rooms flying out at odd angles,
gleaming with militant cheer.
Stripes and dots,
on ironed curtains
and starched pillow cases.
A little sunshine at every turn

of the road,
Menominee, Corpus Christi, Chicago, Alberta,
Bradshaw, Topeka, Emporia, Lincoln, Rockford:
say it again and again
to the children
when they ask where we're going next.
Never had a plan,
just patch the sheets and move on,
wherever the wind blows

around my grandmother's house,
a mobile home,
yet so stationary.
Twenty years ago
she tore the wheels off herself,
and let the scenery pile up like dust
around her strawberry plants.

As I write this I am remembering my own grandmother sitting in her kitchen of forty years ago. She is shelling peas from her garden. The neighbors said she could plant a broomstick and make it grow.

Grandma Rose did most of her kitchen work sitting down. Once, at home, I tried to dry dishes while sitting on a stool, and my mother scolded me. I was only emulating my grandmother. I didn't know then that she was dying of cancer.

I see the potbellied stove she had installed in the corner of her "house in town," although she didn't need it either for warmth or for cooking. It was a legacy of her childhood in France, where she grew up in an unheated farmhouse. I hear her repeating phrases for me in French, translating the childish sentences I invented for her. It was her only opportunity to speak her language; her husband had decreed that only English would be spoken in their household. I remember sleeping overnight in the room under the eaves and waking to the cooing of mourning doves and the tolling of church bells. The memories go on and on. I will have to be very selective. In my poem, I will show her sitting at the kitchen table, shelling the peas and talking to me softly in French. I will bring in her block-long garden and identify the flowers with her. In the closure I will allude to the roses she painted on her cheeks with rouge to spare the family from the reminder that she was dying. Roses and Rose.

☼ FIRESTARTERS

Follow Tina's and Jana's examples in writing a poem about a grandparent. Show him or her at work, either at a job or a labor of love that symbolizes an important character trait. Like Tina, use words or phrases from the grandparent's own language or an American phrase that typifies the person, or, like Jana, use your grandparent's home and surroundings to delineate the person. Your poem will be rich in metaphor and simile, most connected to the task at which your grandparent is working or the home in which your grandparent is living.

Begin by remembering a scene in your mind's eye. Turn up the sound. Is there music? Conversation? Background noise? What are the details of the task? Of the scene? Of the person? How do the two relate? Jot down images; include everything. When you have finished, look over your list and choose only those that fit together and develop the theme. Use the action of the grandparent to propel the poem forward through the consecutive stanzas. You may want to put this poem in your family album.   ☼

COMING TO TERMS

"We write from those places inside us that no one else has."

Tess Gallagher

No subject is inappropriate for poetry, and since poems are born of emotion, they often deal with the most intense experiences, even death. Often, death is hard to accept, especially when it strikes suddenly or takes someone we love. We sometimes write poems to discover how we feel about subjects too emotionally charged to approach through any other means. Poetry relies on an intuitive coherence that helps us find order and sense in events too overwhelming for us to deal with otherwise. We find a measure of comfort in coherence, in understanding how our experience, no matter how difficult, fits into the scheme of things.

A few years ago I watched my mother die slowly from a terminal illness. We could do nothing for this proud and dignified woman beyond making her as comfortable as possible as she regressed to the helplessness of an infant. On an especially bad night, the night before Thanksgiving, she lapsed into semiconsciousness and raised her arms to me, begging for help I was unable to give. Her pleas were exactly the same as those I remembered from my own children, and no doubt the same as those she had once heard from me:

Waiting for Death

I am the mother, she is the child
in the role reversal
of age.
But it's death, not life
that awaits her,
lingering
like a reluctant bridegroom.
She lies on the bed,
a folded sheet like a cinch
holding her in.
The smell of death,
musty as a locked closet,
rises from parchment skin

so fragile it tears
at the slightest touch.
"Help me, help me,"
she whimpers,
supplicant arms extended.
I cradle her to my breast,
whisper senseless reassurance,
"It's all right, I'm here,"
words as empty as "tomorrow,"
words that weight my tongue like stones.

A few months later, Jason Decker's mother died at home, completely unexpectedly. He wrote "Packing" early in his junior year:

Packing

All I have of my mother
lays in a tattered cardboard box.
I lost her once
the day she died,
but I hold her belongings
still.

Now I fold
the fleece, angora, and silk
shells her warmth
once filled.

My hands move slower.
I memorize each piece.
They will leave.
I will lose her
again.

Kevin Mallery lost a close friend very suddenly in an automobile accident. Like many others, he found it difficult to accept her absence. His poignant poem reflects their struggle to reconcile this loss. The Illinois Association of Teachers of English recognized the power of this poem with a First-Place Award:

Good-bye

We call to hear your voice
on the answering machine. Hello,
you say, like you'll be in History
tomorrow. They say good-bye, but I
already told you that after Algebra.
Sitting here in your best friend's bedroom,
I remember the counselor's voice,
"Diana is dead," over and over
like a faucet dripping in the middle of the night,
each drop hitting harder on my mind.
Your mother, so strong at the wake,
like a shoulder to cry on, tells
me how you pouted all night
when she took you home first
from my party in seventh grade,
when we played spin the bottle, and you lost
but didn't care. You lie still
for the first time, your face swollen and scarred, not the
  woman
across the lunch table, a model
since eighth grade. Finally, your mother
cries, "I don't want you to go."
Neither do I, nor he, nor she,
but you lie in a wooden box
six feet from eternity. Your father's
hand reaches to touch your coffin
like a man clutching his throat
in the gas chamber.

☼ FIRESTARTERS

If you have experienced the death of a family member or friend, or encountered any other painful situation, you may find that you can at least make sense of it through poetry. You may feel that the poem is too private to share, in which case you will keep it in your journal; or you may wish to share it with your workshop and others. One of the most human functions of poetry is its gift of connecting us to others, of enabling us to share universal feelings and experience. ☼

USING YOUR FEARS AND PHOBIAS

One of the great compensations for being a poet is that you can turn any significant life experience, no matter how traumatic, into fuel for your writing. Even those fears still lurking in dark corners of your memory can be lured into the light of poetry. You can even reach back into your childhood for ideas. For example, I remember my own nightly ritual of arranging stuffed animals along the edges of my bed and tucking several under the covers with me for insurance. Insurance against what? Why, the monsters who lived under my bed, of course. They were tiny troll-like men who were invisible during the day, but at night they waited under my bed for me to dangle an unwary arm or leg far enough over the side for them to grab, and then. . . .

Before you laugh too hard, think back to your own childhood. Would you actually have walked down the basement stairs at night— alone? How about your closet or the attic? Were you absolutely sure no monsters were hiding there? Did you have to sleep with a night-light on? Or a doll or a teddy bear tucked in beside you? Don't be embarrassed! Use these very normal childhood fears as the groundwork for a poem.

Some of us may have encountered more legitimate fears than the usual childhood bogey men. My son-in-law developed what seemed to be an inexplicable phobia about dolls when he was a toddler. When he was old enough to verbalize, however, he recalled that when he was only two years old, his brother had decapitated a cousin's doll and taunted him with the severed head. You may have a similar story to tell about a phobia of your own. These fears and phobias can become intriguing poems, especially when you relate them to events beyond themselves.

Here is an example from a poem I recently wrote. On a vacation to the Florida keys I finally overcame a long-standing fear of sharks and allowed myself to be drawn into snorkeling in deep water, miles out on the Atlantic Ocean. When I returned safely to land, I began to see how conquering a physical fear can be like taking an emotional risk, and a poem began to take shape. I knew I had to paint the scene in the concrete details of the ocean, so I began by brainstorming. I was pleased to see that so many details could apply at both the literal and metaphorical levels:

dark water
can't see bottom
fear of sharks/danger
cold shock of the water
thrill of the unknown
shadowy shapes
old fears

sudden beauty of an angel fish
silent depths
tug of undertow
pull of seaweed
taste of salt water
choking sensation
coral formations
life invisible from the surface
slow, deep breaths through snorkel
buoyancy of salt water
reassurance of someone I trust
liberation into new world

As I looked at the images above, an order began to arrange itself in my head. I began writing and allowed the images to lead me into the poem. After some revisions, here is the poem that emerged:

Deep Water

For twenty years I've been afraid
of sharks. *Jaws* made me wary
of deep water and dark places
where you can barely discern
shadows gliding ominously
beyond the eyes' perception,
more fear than substance,
a memory in the genetic code
of some primeval ancestor
who even then feared sharks.
Your assurances drew me
into deep water;
and not for the first time,
I plunged in blindly behind you.
Like the other times it began
with an exquisite moment
of panic when I thought I couldn't
breathe and felt myself drowning,
until I saw you there, where you said
you would be. Suddenly, I could
breathe and swim and open myself
as sharp and deeply sensuous
as any we'd entered before.

☼ **FIRESTARTERS**

Use your journal to begin a list of your own fears and phobias. Make this informal. If you can see any links between your old fears and adult issues, jot down the similarities. Here is a brief list of some common fears:

speaking in public	closed spaces
heights	strangers
water	tests
airplanes	darkness
leaving home	worms, spiders, insects

Select a fear or phobia that you have overcome. In a list similar to mine above, parallel the significance of defeating the fear to an element in your current life. Use these images to write a poem, or, alternatively, base your poem on a fear or phobia that you have not conquered. Connect its hold over you as a child to its hold today.   ☼

THE CHANCE REMARK

Once you begin looking and listening to the world as a poet, you will find material for poems everywhere, even in chance remarks. Keep your journal or a small notepad handy to record these windfalls of poetic inspiration.

A few years ago I found a poem hiding in a chance remark by my ophthalmologist, "You don't need bifocals yet." Behind his obvious relief at that fact I sensed an implied conviction that persons who wear bifocals are crossing a line—literally—into middle age. The line dividing bifocal lenses is also the line between youth and middle age. That was a symbol begging for a poem!

The Eye Exam

"You don't need bifocals
yet," the doctor says,
and we both know "yet"
means "coming soon."
"You still look much too young
for bifocals," he says,
relieved to spare us both
that indignity
for another year.
I choose tortoise shell frames,

slightly oversized,
free from lines dividing
youth and middle age.
Chic and secure
for another year,
I fluff my new perm,
checking covertly
for strands of gray,
and tiptoe towards mortality,
blinders securely in place.

Carrie Grzywinski was eating dinner in a restaurant where entertainment was provided by one man in a dark corner playing a guitar. When she said she needed an idea for a poem, her friend said, "Why don't you write about a man playing a guitar?" Her poem was chosen by Gwendolyn Brooks for an Illinois Poet Laureate Award:

Cabaret Guitar

He sits astride
The smoke filled room,
Charming strings
With callused hands,
Overhead lights
Silhouetting his face.
Lips parted, slurring lyrics
Behind deep chords,
He embraces his guitar, like a woman
He'll never have the pleasure
To strum.

Here is a sample of lines from my own journal. Some have already been used in poems; some have turned up in short stories; and some may never be used. The important idea is simply the *listening.* The people around you are an inexhaustible source of ideas:

"Don't ever walk behind an elephant."
"All roads end at the same place."
"Why don't you act your age?"
"That play was obviously written by a man." (regarding Carson McCullers)
"This apartment doesn't *really* look like a rathole."
"Are you accepting gentlemen callers?"

☼ FIRESTARTERS

As you walk through your life of home, school, work, friends, strangers, etc., *listen* to what they say. Jot down interesting remarks in your journal for a poem later. Your own life and your own journal will become an even better source of inspiration because the chance remarks will fit *your* life. Keep paper and pen handy; ideas don't wait for a convenient time!   ☼

POEMS OF SOCIAL CRITICISM

> *"The good poem may be political, but is more interested in enacting or understanding the dynamics of any human situation than it is in effecting change. . . . The poet distracted by the possibility of effecting change is looking too far ahead to be a trustworthy witness of what's in front of him/her. It has been said that a poet must have vision. The good poet's vision is of the here and now. The world, properly seen, becomes the future."*
>
> Steven Dunn

Many young poets use poetry as a means of social criticism, and they are right to do so: poetry has always been involved in politics. Many of our favorite poems are political in nature. For example, "The Pit," by Lucien Stryk, is an unforgettable indictment of war; "Conversation Overheard in a Subway," by Kenneth Fearing, puts all of us on trial for passive guilt; and the "Dream" poems, by Langston Hughes, helped to fuel the civil rights movement. *Anything* intensely felt by the poet is a suitable subject for poetry, so controversial and political topics are certain to emerge . . . and should. However, sometimes the fervor of the political or social conviction causes the writer to forget that poetry is a language of implication, of subtlety. No matter how sincere the message, it should never be delivered with an air hammer. Poetry is never didactic or preachy, for then it would cease to be poetry. The light touch is absolutely necessary. Build your images vividly, and readers will become so involved in the experience that they will draw their own conclusions, which linger long after the closure.

The most effective poems come from the poet's own life, especially when the approach is critical.

When she was a sophomore in high school, my daughter witnessed the horrifying death of a stag deer caused by errors in judgment by public officials we trust to handle emergencies:

Stag

She said he looked like a Dali painting
as he burst through the plate glass,
antlers heavy, eyes wild,
blood framing the canvas.
Behind him, uniformed policemen shouted
and housewives flustered,
their Tuesday routines unhinged
by a stray stag.
Stags don't understand
plate glass,
so when they tried to corner him
against the L-shaped corridor
outside the high school commons,
he panicked and plunged through
all those layers of glass.
He just lay there, quivering
on the polished linoleum,
blood spurting from his nearly severed forelegs
and pooling thickly
into a welcome mat
in front of the principal's office.
My fifteen year old daughter,
who had been alone in the hall
at the moment of impact,
crouched beside him,
her eyes as wide and frightened as his,
as law and order advanced upon them.

Instead of firing a broadside against the conditions of public housing, Kevin Keene wrote this very moving poem:

A'Compte

If I loved you, I would hold
you after love and whisper
across your ear:
"Reveillez-vous coeurs endormis,
Le dieu d'amour vous sonne,"
But
in the projects, I can't speak
Love,
French
or otherwise . . .
you would not understand.

Jean Kern drew on personal experience working with abused children when she wrote "Sacrifice." The poem reflects the cycles of abuse that, unfortunately, run through generations. "Sacrifice" was part of a collection that received an Achievement Award in Writing from the National Council of Teachers of English:

Sacrifice

His skin was clammy,
smelled of urine.
Perfect black eyes
four-soft cheeks,
four-month-old hair that coiled
itself between my fingers.

There was no gentle way
to change his diaper;
his shrieks resounded
as his bruised spine pressed
into hardwood.
I hurried;
envisioned Mommy's clenched
teeth during fits of rage;
hair brushes,
wooden spoons,
belt buckles slamming
into bones soft as petals.

My tears landed
on his brown belly, crawled
between deep purple
ribs. Later they told me
Daddy set Mommy on fire.

☼ FIRESTARTERS

Now try your hand at a poem of social criticism, using implication as
your strongest tool. Choose an issue that concerns you deeply, then
write about it with a subtle touch.   ☼

CHAPTER 8

MAINTAINING THE FIRE:

Poems from People, Places, and Things

"In fact, when retiring for the night and a good fire still remains, cover all of it with ashes from the side of the fireplace. This will hold all night and when uncovered the next day, or even next evening, a good bed of red hot coals will be found upon which a new fire can be laid.

"In this way one can understand how heat and fire were maintained from day to day in the Colonial homes when such fires were a hard necessity."

Raymond W. Dyer,
The Old Farmer's Almanac

POEMS FOR BLACK HISTORY MONTH

Most communities sponsor contests and celebrations during February that invite students to write poems for readings and displays. Good sources of inspiration are the many books compiling pictures and short biographies of great African Americans, books of photographs, and folios of postcards. The visual images that accompany the written commentaries give you natural images on which to focus your poems. Here is a small sampling of important African Americans. (Hint: don't just choose names familiar to you. Some of the lesser-known names have wonderful stories behind them. A few minutes of research can result in remarkable discoveries.)

Malcolm X	Dr. Martin Luther King, Jr.
Mary Church Terrell	Frederick Douglass
W. E. B. DuBois	Mary McLeod Bethune
Arthur Ashe	Rosa Parks
Maya Angelou	Nikki Giovanni
Paul Robeson	Langston Hughes
Louis Armstrong	Leontyne Price
Howlin' Wolf	Odetta
Juanita Hill	Toni Morrison
Jesse Jones	Shirley Chisholm
Jesse Jackson	Marva Collins
Dr. Marjorie S. Joyner	Lena Horne
Charlie Parker	James Baldwin
Coretta Scott King	Carol Moseley Braun
James Meredith	Harriet Tubman
Sojourner Truth	Catherine Harris
Scott Joplin	Ada S. McKinley
Bessie Smith	Gwendolyn Brooks
Guion S. Bluford, Jr.	Mary Hatwood Futrell

Another source for your poems is your own reading. Think of poems, short stories, essays, and novels that have affected you and your thinking. During his sophomore and junior years, Kevin Keene read deeply and widely in Black literature, especially Black poetry. He grew increasingly concerned that so much of the work deals with the oppressive hold the past still maintains over so many Americans. During the spring of his junior year, he added his voice to those of other young Black poets who refuse to be shackled by old chains.

Kevin had been greatly affected by reading Ralph Ellison's *The Invisible Man* and agreed with Ellison's belief that inside each of us there is an "invisible" person who supersedes skin color and the world's perception of our outside appearances. Kevin's most striking image, the red blood common to both Blacks and Whites, runs throughout the poem. His other pervasive image, the crow, shoots off into many directions, adopting varying connotations, all involved in Black history. The form here is a modern sonnet, appropriate for Kevin's serious tone and complex subject. This sonnet shows how you can make the restrictions of formal verse work for you in creating a memorable poem. "Soul Owner" was part of a collection that earned Kevin recognition from the Arts Talent Search of the National Foundation for Advancement in the Arts:

Soul Owner

If you stab me, I will not scream. My blood
runs red as yours, yet the rift clots our paths.
The fissure cracks through us—shrill crows of hell-
bent loss. I am resilient as the crow.

I am resilient. Let us shoot down black
bird Birmingham, Selma, Montgomery,
as wound bolls birth white, twist from blood, and fall.
So I read failure in Our poetry.

I read failure: proud ones drowned in wine, drunken
over white laws in Africa. My shackles
on the boat remain: scarce, empty, and broken.
Cast far from my soul, far outside my skin.

Skinless, color is of no value, as
silken feathers ochre tipped—the blood dries slow.

Kevin Mallery wrote a caustic free verse poem aimed at those whose prejudice led to the assassination of Dr. Martin Luther King, Jr.:

Doctor King

Silence him.
If you hear him,
he'll sit with you,
drink with you,
share his knowledge with you.
Choose to shackle him to the wall,

he won't fight back with a sword;
his tongue cuts deeper than any blade.
He speaks the words
of millions, he dreams
the dreams of millions.
You still don't hear the message,
but a bullet through his dream
can't stop it.
It's contagious:
don't catch the disease
of thinking his blood
runs red as yours.
He's not like you:
he's black, you're white,
she's brown, you're not,
but we're all yellow.
To be different,
we crucify him.

Sound is an intrinsic part of poetry, so you may listen to Black music to begin your poem: spirituals, jazz, blues, or rap. You may have noticed in reading Black poets that much of their work follows the rhythms and patterns of Black music. For example, Langston Hughes was deeply influenced by the sounds of jazz, and his poetry is infused with its sounds. Gillen Mowry discovered her poem in the sound of spirituals. Repetition forms a natural frame for this poem just as it does in most spirituals:

Go Tell

Elijah, he sings, ee lie ie jah!
Mouth eating sky, chest leather
Bared, voice a shackle for the whip
Which crossed his flesh.
The song rolls off as sweat.
Sun blistered shoulder splits
With metal plow turned to earth. Bolls of white
Cotton bloody hand and railroaded
Backs bend to hell, digging
Ditches under the sun, burnt
Into the ground and memory of white
Washed crosses, remembering stillness

And animal sounds from a place
As dark and free as they
Aren't now, singing Elijah,
eee lie ie jah.

☀ FIRESTARTERS

Through your own reading, research, or interest in Black music, compose your own poem for Black history month. You may choose the dignity of form as in Kevin Keene's sonnet, the informality of Kevin Mallery's free verse, or the musical influence of Gillen Mowry's poem. In any case, your subject will determine your approach.   ☀

POEMS FROM PAINTINGS: *Edward Hopper*

Poems and paintings are drawn from the same roots and are probably closer in approach than any other art forms. They both ask and answer the same questions. They draw on emotion, intuition, and implication. They are created and executed according to the same considerations. These are points that Edward Hirsch, Poet in Residence at The Art Institute of Chicago, reiterates each time he works with student poets. His whole focus is the correlation of art and poetry.

A poem, like a painting, must have a definite sense of time and place; it must project a mood, be told from a particular perspective and through a particular voice. Both the painting and the poem must imply a narrative, presenting certain carefully chosen details and holding others as secrets. Both must be thematically consistent; that is, the details must all work toward the same effect, the same central tension. Finally, the painting and the poem must be approached first from the literal level, the level of all human experience, before they may be considered figuratively. The concrete details, the sensory images, are the language of both the painter and the poet.

Study a print of *Nighthawks at the Diner,* by Edward Hopper (1942), carefully, asking yourself questions and writing the answers as notes for your poem. Thematically, this poem seems to deal with isolation, perhaps even desolation. How is this theme projected?

Setting: There is a definite sense of time and place—urban America, in the early hours of the morning. What time is it in your mind? Where is the diner?

Approach: The effect here is like a fishbowl with you, the viewer, looking in. Everything outside the diner is dark; the only light visible seems to be filtering out from the inside. The light is garish, artificial, intended to cast a particular feeling onto the coffee drinkers. What is that feeling? Look at the store across the street. What do you see? Isn't this an odd store, with no wares? The only light here comes from the diner.

Now consider some of the other details outside of the diner. There is no debris in the streets, no sign that humans have ever passed here. Isn't this detail unrealistic in a painting that is executed in a carefully realistic manner? Note the geometric exactness, the true-to-life believability of the diner, even down to the reflections off the counter. How are the reflections important?

Consider the figures inside the diner. Note how no one touches; no one looks at anyone else. The couple seems to be together yet alone. What is the effect of the light reflecting on their faces? Did you notice that there are no doors to the outside? What might that imply? The man and woman are drinking coffee; what else are they doing? The man sitting alone is even more mysterious; only his back is in view. What do the details of his clothing and posture indicate? Who are these people; why are they here? Only the man behind the counter has an obvious reason to be there: he is working, earning a wage. How might he view the nighthawks?

Technique: Notice how smooth the brush strokes are. Hopper has taken care to give this painting an almost photographic smoothness. Why? How might you duplicate this effect in words?

Title: As in a poem, the title of a painting can be a great help to the viewer. Why did Hopper title this painting *Nighthawks?* Aren't people usually called night owls? What are the differences between a hawk and an owl? What implications might be projected here? How are the people like hawks? Since this is the title of the painting, you will want to consider this question in detail.

I did this assignment along with my class. The title of the poem also serves as the first line, an idea you may wish to try:

Three A.M.: The Woman in Red

drinks coffee and waits
for first light.
The man beside
her drinks coffee and chain smokes.
The smoke drifts
into her face;
she knows he knows
how she hates it,
almost more than she hates sitting
here with him.
The woman in red
drinks coffee and picks at her nails,
flaking red lacquer islands
onto a formica sea.
Off the walls light
reflects, the garish yellow
of nightmares and illness,
the color she feels
inside.
The man beside
her blows smoke
the color of the walls.
She feels it enter
the pores of her skin,
the chambers of her heart.
She coughs, he lights
another cigarette.
Beside him she dreams
of dawn rising
in thin red puffs
beyond the horizon.

Michelle Van Ness wrote a poem that became part of the collection that earned her an award from the National Foundation for Advancement in the Arts. Notice the smooth narrative effect of the interlocking stanzas:

She Is the Nighthawk

She is the nighthawk who picks
her nails at 3 A.M.
brown coffee swallowing
cheap sugar,
perched on her stool
with Norman and his Marlboro
barely glowing in his fingers shaking
as they rise to his mouth, linear clouds
of smoke curling around
his hat like her arms
the time she hugged him
after finishing
research in jungles
of concrete projects
the time his arms trembled
on her shoulders
like the old man downstairs
waiting to help with her coat

that hides her red dress
and white collarbone under
scarlet waves resting
at the counter, she waits
for bubbles of cream to pop.

Our class used other Hopper prints as alternative prompts for this assignment. The results were some of the best poems written that year. Kevin Mallery used *Summer Evening* (1947) as inspiration for his poem. The image of the freight train reverberates through the second half of the poem like wheels of boxcars clicking over metal rails at night:

Summer's Over

He's coming over you yell
as you run to the bathroom
leaving the phone off the hook.
Curlers, makeup, you even shave your legs.
Your mother
doesn't ask, she doesn't need to,

you only get this way for him.
He pulls up in his Mustang,
and before he knocks, you're out the door
On the porch, you get close
but he pushes you away.
We need to talk, he says.
I'm sorry, he says,
it's over.
My God you think.
His words
race through your head
like a freight train,
over and over you hear
him tell you. He goes on,
but you look away, listening only
to his voice in your head.
Trapped on your porch,
the searchlight of a train
bearing down on you
until it runs you over.

Judith Lloyd wrote an intriguing poem from *Chop Suey* by Edward Hopper. She manages to take the poem into a mystical dimension even beyond the painting. In her first draft, Judy had a much longer poem. At my suggestion she cut the first half off entirely, realizing that it was just warm-up for what she *really* wanted to say. Unlike essays, poems don't need—or want—introductions. They live an intense life of their own—immediately.

mirror image

you tell me we all have one double
somewhere in the world one person
who dresses and moves and breathes
just as you do one person
with my blue hat and black clothing
one person with your green clothing
and black hat you tell me we all
have one double and she is the same
she is left handed she speaks
in the same low tone
she is watching another double
behind another blue bowl
and another teapot

sometimes as you raise your right
hand to your mouth as i raise my left
i squint my right eye to see
your squinting left eye better
i see us trapped on either side
of a one-way mirror watching you
dream of your double
and wish you could meet her
in unspoken synchronicity
we blink in time

Judy has chosen some interesting poetic techniques here. The line breaks are perfect; the absence of capitalization works, and instead of punctuation, she has used spaces between thoughts. This form will work only in a poem as tightly written as this, where ideas flow into one another as naturally as these doubles and their *doppelgangers*.

Ridgely Dunn also based her poem on *Chop Suey*, but took an entirely different approach. This poem won first place in *Poet* magazine's high school competition:

The Town Next to China

She is the exception to the rule I made
about making friends with women whose smiles melt plastic.
I'm going to prove I'm steel, like a teapot, stainless
exotic as jasmine
I will fool her with complexity, seeming sparse.
She will stop noticing the little things:
the way my trench coat is a separate person
and when I take it off, I cannot hide in shadow
and thus invent my own.

Her face is finding sunlight
in the red glow of the neon sign next door.
Her skull is shaped by outside influences,
the hat she wears like a challenge, fortune cookies in her
    purse.
I am as empty as the table behind us
and when she speaks I find my darkness.

☼ FIRESTARTERS

For this assignment you will need an Edward Hopper poster book purchased from an art store or an art book from the library containing

Edward Hopper's paintings. Then, to create your poem, you will need to cover the same considerations as a painter. You will want to include all of the techniques available to poets and painters. Run through your notes and select only those details that will present the effect you choose. In addition, you will use two tools that were not available to Hopper; you will choose a narrative voice and weave a narrative *from what you see and imagine* in the painting. Whatever psychology or story you project into the poem must be completely consistent with the literal details of the painting. Remember: you must select the images for the literal level before you can consider the figurative level. Concrete details are the only language in which to discuss abstract ideas; if you attend carefully to the details, the theme will develop itself. Your closure will become the line of general implication that pulls the poem together and throws your reader into possibilities and discoveries beyond the words themselves. Implication is your language and Hopper's.   ✻

MORE POEMS FROM PAINTINGS

After you have done the Edward Hopper assignment in the preceding section, you can easily apply the same approach to other paintings. Ask yourself some of the same questions, consider the same perspectives. Art feeds on art; the genres are all related: that's why you so often find creative people interested in more than one medium of expression. Mark Strand and John Updike are just two of the many poets who earned degrees in art. Even those writers who do not draw or paint love art. Hemingway may have been more than half serious when he claimed he learned to write from viewing Impressionist paintings in the Louvre.

All during high school, Aaron Anstett had been intrigued by Edvard Munch's *The Scream* and had previously tried to write about it. Finally, he wrote a poem about trying to write about it:

I've tried so many times

to write a poem for Munch's *The Scream*
of 1895 that I feel like the guy inside it,
you know, the one in so much pain
he could rip his head off
push up on those hands
over each ear

to stop himself from hearing.
everything's at such an impossible angle
the bridge he's about to jump off of

the lines like scratches in the sky
and that body twisted as a wick
with everything about to go out.
in two minutes he'd run right at us
still holding on to his skull
but he's trapped screaming there forever
with two boats on the water
and two gentlemen at the end of the bridge
walking towards the vanishing point,
the one with his head turned back slightly
wishing that man
would just shut up.

Kerry Santoro chose a huge painting by Georges Seurat done in pointillism, showing a variety of people enjoying Sunday afternoon in a park along the Seine. Kerry focused her poem on just one of the intriguing figures:

A Girl on the Island of La Grande Jatte

Like a Persian cat, she glares
at me. Her eyes glaze
over my dark reflections
through glass,
the pond, a mirror
of shadows stretching
from my magnetic stare.
The sun beats
upon her back,
drowning black silhouettes
into the lawn.

Wanchay Chanthadouangsy created a dramatic narrative for Reginald Marsh's *Tattoo and Haircut*. She speaks from the perspective of one of the figures, a rough-looking man who operates a barber shop/ tattoo parlor:

A Clean Towel to Every Customer

It might be days, even weeks
leaning against the door,
splinters like needles in our backs,
'til a drunken sailor or some tough teenager,
arm draped over a girlfriend off the street,
staggers into our shop
and says "Hey you, I want
an eagle" and points to his chest
"and a heart that says 'I love Joe'
on the thigh for my girl."
Or sometimes "Gimme the skull
and crossbones." He slides black
leather off his shoulders,
"Make me look tough."
These days are lucky,
and we take special care
to sterilize the needle.
We mix new green ink
'til it's the color of snakes,
rose leaves and feathers.
Sometimes the customer
wants red or yellow,
we mix colors 'til
they're hearts and sunshine
But we can't offer no pain—
a tattoo hurts like
bullets scraping your shoulders
or jackknives scarring your chest.
The pain pulses,
insistent and burning after
we pierce your skin
and let the paint shoot in
holes 'til it flows under, connects in lines.
At first they look like poison
but they won't kill ya.
Tattoos are badges
sayin' you've earned it,

you've been through
it all like the time
you jumped ship to save
your friend or stabbed
a cop who thought you stole
some money. Before, you were no one,
a sailor with no medals, no stripes.
We can give you
rewards and dreams.
We can even give you a life,
and in the process,
a clean towel.

☼ FIRESTARTERS

Put your imagination to work creating poems around paintings. Ideally, you should try to visit an art museum and study the paintings themselves. If that is impossible, however, you may use a poster book, postcard booklet, or any of the art books available in libraries or bookstores. Here is a list of some of the painters and paintings you might use for inspiration:

Vincent Van Gogh	*Self Portrait 1886/87, The Bedroom 1888*
Lyonel Feininger	*Carnival in Arcueil*
Georges Seurat	*A Sunday on La Grande Jatte*
Gustave Caillebotte	*Paris, a Rainy Day*
Georgia O'Keeffe	*Cebolla Church*
Grant Wood	*American Gothic*
Mary Cassatt	*The Bath*
Pablo Picasso	*Mother and Child*
Paul Delvaux	*The Village of the Mermaids*
Henri de Toulouse-Lautrec	*At the Moulin Rouge*
Reginald Marsh	*Tattoo and Haircut*
Edvard Munch	*The Scream*

These are just suggestions on where to begin. Choose any art source of interest to you and allow your imagination to roam.   ☼

POEMS FROM PHOTOGRAPHS: A Lesson from Garrett Hongo

The Hongo Store
29 Miles Volcano
Hilo, Hawaii
From A Photograph

My parents felt those rumblings
Coming deep from the earth's belly,
Thudding like the bell of the Buddhist Church.
Tremors in the ground swayed the bathinette
Where I lay squalling in soapy water.

My mother carried me around the house,
Back through the orchids, ferns, and plumeria
Of that greenhouse world behind the store,
And jumped between gas pumps into the car.

My father gave it the gun
And said, "Be quiet," as he searched
The frequencies, flipping for the right station
(The radio squealing more loudly than I could cry.)

And then even the echoes stopped—
The only sound the Edsel's grinding
And the bark and crackle of radio news
Saying stay home or go to church.

"Dees time she no blow!"
My father said, driving back
Over the red ash covering the road.
"I worried she went go for broke already!"

So in this print the size of a matchbook,
The dark skinny man, shirtless and grinning,
A toothpick in the corner of his smile,
Lifts a naked baby above his head—
Behind him the plate glass of the store only cracked.

Garrett Hongo was inspired to write this poem because of a tiny snapshot of his father swinging him as an infant over his head in a gesture of relief and victory. Attached to that photo, of course, was the story of the abortive volcano: how Hongo's mother snatched him from his bathinette and joined her husband in an escape that easily could have been doomed if the volcano erupted. Behind the father and son is the store window. That cracked window sets up the whole story.

Kelly Boske also looked at a photograph for inspiration. Hers was not a family photo; instead, it showed a young woman trying on a new dress. Like Hongo, Kelly anchors her poem to concrete details, all surrounding an embroidered flower:

Ai dio

In Saigon fingers strain
over tulips embroidered
by hands proud as new fathers.
A thousand years of ancestry
preserved in every stitch.

In the mirror the dress
tugs at her neck,
clings to her shoulders
like a child,
Heritage
draping her face
in fine black hair.
She traces fingers along buttons
aligned like garden rows
from waist to neck,
rubs fabric
cool and smooth as petals
across her skin.
She brings the flower
to her cheek
and presses hard,
Hoping to make an imprint
preserving a thousand years.

☼ FIRESTARTERS

Using a photograph as a prompt, write your own poem, either about someone you know or about a stranger. Look in old photograph albums, yearbooks, photography books, your grandmother's attic— anywhere you might find intriguing photographs. Use the photographic image as the framework of your poem. Like Hongo, you will want to find a photo with a sense of story, ideally represented by something as concrete as the cracked store window. Then write your poem, using either family history or your own imagination to fill in the narrative. Connect the story line to something concrete in the photograph: a uniform, an article of clothing, a toy, a pet, a car, a cane, a missing tooth, a suitcase, a gift, whatever.

Remember that your poem requires an appropriate setting. Look back at "The Hongo Store" and list the concrete details that paint the backdrop for the story. What images show the scene to be Hawaii and the time a generation ago? What tangible details relate the parents' emotions throughout the incident? You will want to include similar details in your own poem to give it emotional texture.

Don't be afraid to let your people talk. What they say and how they say it can only add to the fullness of the picture. Hongo's father speaks only a few words, but look what those words show! First, urgency; then relief; and the broken English of this young man is especially endearing. We want him to endure; we suddenly *care* about his family. What kind of courage or tenacity permits him to live at the base of a volcano? Without allowing Hongo's father his own words, the picture would be fuzzy.

This assignment calls for only one poem from a photograph, but you could easily write a collection of poems using photographs as a motif. Return to this lesson whenever you begin to worry that the well is running dry. You'll find poems rising to the surface whenever you need them.   ☼

POEMS FROM TELEVISION

We frequently read that television robs children of their imagination. The charge is undoubtedly true for children who spend far too much time sitting passively in front of a TV. However, a generation of new poets is moving into prominence, all of whom grew up with TV, so it would appear that television in moderation is not especially harmful. In fact, it can even be the inspiration for your own poems. Think back to the programs you watched when you were growing up, the programs you watch now. Already, ideas for poems are starting to multiply, aren't they?

I grew up with *Howdy Doody, Mickey Mouse Club, I Love Lucy, The Lone Ranger, Superman,* and *Father Knows Best.* Father no longer knows best if we look to Al Bundy or Homer Simpson as models. Can you see the material for poetry inside the cultural changes represented by this complete reversal of paternal respect?

Aaron Anstett grew up with *The Brady Bunch, Speed Racer, The Partridge Family, The Monkees, Lost in Space,* and professional wrestling. He mined those childhood television memories to write "Claw":

Claw

The big-time wrestler Baron von Claw
fought normal the first couple rounds
and should have lost. He was older, and his belly showed
under his tights. He had to be fifty, a little fat guy
who got thrown around. But something always happened

across his face. Done for, his eyes changed,
pushed out of their sockets a bit and widened
like stains. About to be pinned, he'd be let up. Ali Baba,
Texas Jack, these powerful men would just unhand him,
simply stop fighting as the Baron stood upright,

and look around nervous and inch away backwards.
It was then always, that the camera zoomed in
on the Baron's lips, which trembled a long time
before he said the word *Claw. Claw,* he'd say,
Claw, and next to his grin the Baron's right hand

would flash up, menacing, all five fingers cramped
and hideous, tips pointed straight at the camera
and the whole screen full of those tips.
When the camera pulled back the Baron's start staggering
behind his claw, as if it led him. He took his time

pacing the ring. Even the announcers never blamed
King Henry, Mr. Insane, for giving in, for begging and
  cowering,
blubbering *No. No.* as the claw descended. It did bad things.
It made a man nothing. The Baron himself would black out in
  spasms
if, before it went, he clasped his hands together, champion.

✺ FIRESTARTERS

Look back to your own childhood for television memories to make your own poems. Here is a partial list of some popular series you may remember:

Silver Spoon	*Speed Racer*
The Brady Bunch	*Bozo's Circus*
The Partridge Family	*Eight Is Enough*
Rocky and Bullwinkle	*Three's Company*
Star Trek: The Next Generation	*Miami Vice*
Family Ties	*Happy Days*
Facts of Life	*The Jeffersons*
Sesame Street	*Laverne and Shirley*
Different Strokes	*Magnum, P.I.*
Dallas	*Dynasty* ☼

POEMS ABOUT LITERARY FIGURES

Sooner or later, most poets find themselves writing about other writers. This is only natural, since writing feeds on writing, and poets, like other writers, recognize their enormous debts to those whose work has influenced them. In fact, it is absolutely essential that young writers spend time learning about the lives, the work, and the creative processes of other writers. My advice is to select a writer and read the work intensively. Read and talk to others about the writer, until he or she becomes as real and as close to you as any of your friends. Then move on to another and follow the same process. This approach is much more effective than reading randomly from anthologies. You will learn best from intensive study of successful writers, one at a time. One by one, they will yield the secrets of their particular gifts, and your own style will evolve, based mainly on you, of course, but influenced and polished by the writers you have read.

Michelle Van Ness read all of Raymond Carver's short stories and most of his poems. After viewing a film biography of Carver, a photo of Carver as a boy stuck in her mind. In his troubled brow she saw the inevitability of the alcoholism he would battle and defeat as an adult. The next twelve years were the best in his life: he composed some of the most influential stories and poems of recent years, married poet Tess Gallagher, and, sadly, died of lung cancer in 1988. At a Chicago reading, Michelle presented this poem to Tess Gallagher:

Ray

Flat feet buckled
into Buster Browns
he squats,
knees poking
out of overalls

One finger scratches
the mud
rivulets following
the fingertip
pointing ahead
to frosted mornings
blanketing
drunken nights,
cheeks pushing
up, black crescents
squint
at the camera,
brows furrowed
into one groove.

Sean McDowell started writing largely because he studied Ernest Hemingway during his sophomore year in high school. As a senior he wrote a tribute to Hemingway, reflecting the author's concern for writing the truth and his condemnation of those who betray truth for money:

Kilimanjaro

"The marvelous thing is that
it's painless," he said. "That's how you
know when it starts."
It's already started,
painless or not, and the grease
from the production line soils
my hands, my clothes, my eyes,
my mind.

It's not quite as holy as
gangrene,
but just as effective,
as we put in 8, 10, 11
hour shifts for pennies,
dirty ones at that, while
the others make gold flow
from their fingertips, using
faulty parts and shoddy craftsmanship.
Sorry, fellas, no rebates here.
You bought it, you're stuck with it,
can't afford a guarantee.

There's no snow to find myself
or something else in, and
Kilimanjaro's just too far
away.

Tracy Bushman was also deeply affected by reading Ernest Hemingway. She used him as a point of reference in a poem about a close friend,
another writer in our workshop. The sophisticated allusions in this
poem earned her recognition as runner-up in high school competition
through *Poet* magazine:

You Thought You Knew Hemingway

You try to explain,
call him a drunk and a lunatic until
sarcasm dies halfway up Kilimanjaro.
Still you make me laugh. A soldier's tale
in an Italian ambulance.
You never care.
Write conflict into your stories. You need some.
A bull fight.
A code of ethics.
A bottle of whiskey or NyQuil
on the bedside table.
Hemingway lost his mind, one day.
That would be the way to go.
I mean, I'm me with you, but not always
with me. You can't help it, you
say. Nurses make you feel better.

Is something else wrong?
You told me to check the nut
behind the wheel, then stole words
back. Your stories never have endings,
just character. A voice rattles in minds,
wakes sleeping friends
with a shotgun blast.
You know me.
I'm a hunter
in my mind. No bottle under my pillow.
I need something else. That's old news,
you mutter. Drink absinthe,
everything's licorice
after a while.

Keep talking
about Infinity and Intoxication
and hope for a short happy life.

Susan Carbajal's life has been deeply affected by Gwendolyn Brooks. When Susan was a junior, she heard Brooks read; a few days later, she drafted a poem about the experience. At a reception at our school in honor of Brooks, Susan was finally able to meet the poet who meant so much to her, and she was able to read the final version of her poem:

The Reading
For Gwendolyn Brooks

Your voice fills the auditorium, doubles your height.
You clutch the podium, feet bolted to the floor,
edges of your skirt rippling.
Silence fills the space
between a comma and a word.

Your poems don't drip with roses or clichés
when you talk about abortion
You speak of friends on shelves,
draw pictures with your words.
You use your life to cement images
like the legs of a bench to the floor.
I whimper with Lincoln West,
remember tendrils of my own hair
tangling like weeds in gardens of the More Acceptable.

When your words end, your body stops moving.
Admiring hands flood the air hoping
to find the meaning of life,
the sources of your inspiration.
I slouch in my seat, wonder
who you love, what you eat for dinner, afraid
of being passed over for a better question.

☼ FIRESTARTERS

Write a poem of tribute to an influential writer in your life, or, as Tracy did, use allusions from the life and work of a celebrated writer to add a polished layer of comparison to someone you know. In either case, be certain to select accurate details to create the effect you choose.   ☼

POEMS ABOUT LITERATURE

By this point you are well aware that writers are readers, and you have no doubt done some serious reading of your own. While enjoying the reading and learning style from the writers, you have also added to the well of your own poetic inspiration. The more you read, the more you will find to write about. You will see how situations and emotions in the literature you read reflect your own life. Soon you will find yourself alluding naturally to these works as you write your own poems. You may even decide to write a poem about a piece of literature itself. Nearly every poet does.

One of Ray Bradbury's novels, *Death Is a Lonely Business,* begins with the ghosts of abandoned trolley cars at Venice Beach plunging off the end of the track into the ocean. Shortly after reading the book, I used that image in a poem. In my poem, the speaker finds himself figuratively racing downhill to oblivion, appropriately in one of Bradbury's trolley cars:

A Lonely Business

Death
is a lonely business
like Life
when you're riding
that last trolley
downhill to oblivion.
The tracks are rough,
traveled today
only by apparitions
of cars
hurtling themselves
blindly
into the sea.
Alone
in the back
of the dimly lit
car, you careen
into that last wide
curve,
fear closing like a vice
in the pit of your stomach
as you see straight
ahead in the dark
that razor sharp descent.

After reading *Paco's Story* by Larry Heineman, a novel about a man who had been maimed both physically and emotionally in Vietnam, Michelle Khazai wrote "AWOL":

AWOL

for Paco

Awake, the bits and pieces of flesh
      scrambled like eggs over the jungle
      seep into his mind like the blood
      on Bluebeard's key
At home, the eyes (blue brown cold as steel)
      he scrubs raw his hands and face and heart
      and the blood vanishes
      only to appear on the other side.
At the diner, he picks up the soap, the towel
      picks up the casserole dish
      rubs and rinses 12 hours a day
      every night he fumbles for the gnarled cane,
      leaning heavily
      energy burned up like a July 5 firecracker
Asleep, dreams weave his sheets into spirals
      of cold sweat and booby traps
      that let him kill in two places at once
He leaves. "There's less bullshit the farther west you go."

☀ FIRESTARTERS

Make a list of the stories, poems, novels, that have affected you. Which of them touches your own life? Which of them could you write a poem about, as Michelle did in "AWOL"? Whichever option you choose, begin with a list of images, then fill in the gaps for coherence. ☀

BORROWING A FIRST LINE

How often have you read an absolutely wonderful first line of a poem and wished you had written it? Here's an idea that gives you a second chance. Simply borrow a memorable first line from a poem you admire, and write the rest of the poem yourself. When you are finished, either dedicate the poem to the poet who wrote the line or change the first line to something original, and you'll have a poem of your own design.

Another approach is to choose an intriguing first line from a poem you *haven't* read. This alternative ensures that your poem will not be influenced in theme or form by the original poet's ideas. You must still either dedicate the poem to the original poet (those are still his/her words!) or change your first line. Some remarkable first lines are listed below. Your teacher may have some additional suggestions.

"This was your very first wall, your crib against"

> Norman Dubie, "Comes Winter, the Sea Hunting"

"Taut on the leash, at last I have my way:"

> Alfred Corn, "Moving: New York-New Haven Line"

"I buried Mama in her wedding dress"

> Ai, "She Didn't Even Wave"

"Silent, my jaws working, I knew"

> Paul Mariani, "The Lesson"

"An egg won't roll well"

> William Matthews, "An Airplane Breakfast"

"Something has happened to my name"

> Naomi Shihab Nye, "Catalogue Army"

"There is nothing you can say to a man who drinks."

> Stephen Ortiz, "The Drunken Man"

"Summer is a chartreuse hell in the mountains"

> Molly Peacock, "Old Roadside Resorts"

"At the bad time, nothing betrays the harsh findings"

Robert Pinsky, "December Blues"

☼ FIRESTARTERS

Choose a line from the list above or another source, and let your imagination run. You can begin with an intuitive freewriting, a list of images, or just start writing line by line to see what happens. You can be certain of one thing: the poem you create will be entirely different from the one whose first line you borrowed. ☼

POEMS BASED ON ODDITIES

Aaron Anstett had read a bit of trivia that he couldn't quite forget: an octopus has three hearts. He couldn't leave it alone. Does an octopus *know* it has three hearts? Are the hearts located inside its head? How can three hearts decide who controls eight legs? Do all three hearts die at the same time? Finally, Aaron succumbed to the itch and wrote a poem about it, a lighthearted beginning that eventually became one of the poems *Shenandoah* selected to publish:

Slow Learners

We imagine the octopus knows
nothing of his three hearts or how
some day they'll give out, one by one.
When the eyes are closed, the eight legs done
curling up like pilots who pass out
at those high altitudes, the hearts take turns
getting cold. What a horrible thing to think
all day and night of the octopus
and his three hearts in his fat head.
They keep to themselves mostly,
but sometimes whisper answers
to each other like children
in a school for slow learners.

When he was in middle school, Sean Dempsey had purchased a book at the used book sale held annually by our local library. It was the 1964 third edition of *Oddities: A Book of Unexplained Facts* by a (then elderly) English gentleman named Rupert T. Gould. I know he was elderly because the first edition of this book was printed in 1923. I also know he was elderly because of the circumspect language he used in discussing such oddities as "The Devil's Hoof-Marks," "The Planet Vulcan," and "The Berbalangs of Cagayan Sulu." Sean was especially intrigued by the Berbalangs, humans who, according to Filipino legend, leave their bodies to assume the form of fireflies in order to enter the bodies of their victims and feed upon their entrails:

The Berbalangs of Cagayan Sulu

Certain citizens
quit their bodies
as insects.
Fireflies.
Their body splits
and pours out black.

My brother says he's seen them,
swarming from windows.
You salt their skins,
and wait until they return
to find ill fitting bodies.
This kills them.

I've never liked bugs,
thick in heat,
tangled in my hair.
I smashed
the firefly lanterns
we made as children,
smeared them in glowing trails.

What do Aaron's octopus and Sean's Berbalangs have in common? They are both oddities fortunate enough to have been read by a poet. Most people would have said, "Weird!" and forgotten them. Aaron and Sean thought about it, asked themselves questions, and looked beneath the surface of an appealing oddity. The result, of course, was two poems totally original in their insight and perception.

☼ FIRESTARTERS

Think back over your own reading. What little oddities do you remember? What seemingly useless trivia have you been storing either in your memory or in your journal? Try some brainstorming of images or a freewriting to see whether you have the makings of a poem filed away in your memory.

Go to the library and consult any of the many books of trivia, oddities, anomalies, and world records. You will find enough material there for a whole collection of poems. I recently wrote a poem inspired by the band Devo, who believe that people are de-evolving into potatoes. What poet with a sense of humor can allow a statement like that to slip away? Use your journal to record a list of possibilities for future poems.

POEMS ABOUT WRITING

Writers write what they know. Therefore, one day soon it is likely that you will want to write a poem about writing. You're in good company. Most poets have at some time or another put pen to paper to write about the writing process. It stands to reason: something that commands so much of your time and energy should ultimately become the subject of a poem.

We all know that although the result of our work may be rewarding, the process itself may be torture. Susan Carbajal was recently awarded an Illinois Poet Laureate Award from Gwendolyn Brooks for her poem about the agony of writing. (I think I recognize a reference to my red pen.)

Toils

Etching words in stone,
sweat rolls down her face like raindrops
from storms clouding her brain.
Clutching the pen
between fingers yearning
for the smooth touch of a basketball,
she pushes words from her pen
like lemmings off a cliff.
Red ink drenches black,
filling deserted margins with words,
coaxing images paralleled with reality.
She wipes her brow, sweat dripping from her hand
like water from a soaked rag.
Hands shaking, she places pen on paper.
One eye shut, she searches truth,
expecting a grade.

That last line says it all, doesn't it? What do teachers ask of students? Total honesty, artistic commitment; and then teachers give students a grade.

In a poem that was part of his Scholastic portfolio collection, Peter Noback worried that he could be lured away from ink and paper by the electronic lure of technology:

Hunger

Can I survive
on meals of ink and paper?
I am an animal cursed
with this insatiable appetite.

I prey upon my own senses,
desires for pulsating lights and neon,
gorge myself on junk food visions,
solitary confinement in electronic switches.

I can't break the chains of impulse,
the day is wrapped in Styrofoam.
There's a dying voice within me,
drowned in the roar of digital flesh.

Conscience shot with Novocain,
my eyes glow at night.
Am I infected with a new virus,
black plague of these Dark Ages?

My mind currents and magnets
charged by these basic instincts,
like Pavlov's dogs, hunger
forever ringing bells in my head.

Ridgely Dunn shows that she is serious about poetry in a poem filled with allusions to Emily Dickinson, Sylvia Plath, and Anne Sexton. She places herself among the women who dare to write real poems about strength and certainty and sisterhood, and about truth, even when it is unpleasant:

Validation

We will bury Emily
without honors.
Sisters by the graveside of sappy,
sentimental poetry.

We expect no headstones,
no rhyming tribute.
We are too exotic for tradition.
Our spindly vines ensnare
the Daddy's girls.
Nightshade in our tea,
we are immune to all words
but our own.

Yes, sentences should all begin with I,
speak of shadow, kinship, and roses,
not delicately, like a slippered princess.
But with symbols of motherhood,
Amazon war and blood.
Doom shouldn't be disguised
by blooming fragrances.
That is not the duty of poetry
or women.

☼ FIRESTARTERS

You can return to this assignment again and again, since your perception of the role of the writer is likely to change from one year to another. Where does writing figure in your life? What are its joys, its agonies? To which poets do you feel kinship? What drives you to write? How has writing affected your life?   ☼

> "Even though we learn how to construct a hot and economical fire, I am not sure the lover of an open fire is out of the woods yet. One still will have to hope his favorite ecologist will forgive and forget the little smoke that curls from the chimney."
>
> Raymond W. Dyer, *The Old Farmer's Almanac*

Acknowledgments

Booth, Phillip: From *Letter from a Distant Land.* © 1957. Published by Viking.

Carver, Raymond: "At Night the Salmon Move" by Raymond Carver. Reprinted by permission of Tess Gallagher. © 1983 by Tess Gallagher.

Castillo, Ana: From *My Father Was a Toltec.* Copyright © 1995 by Ana Castillo. Published by W. W. Norton & Co. and originally published in somewhat different from by West End Press in 1988.

Clifton, Lucille: "miss rosie" copyright © 1987, by Lucille Clifton. Reprinted from *Good Woman: Poems and a Memoir 1969–1980,* by Lucille Clifton, with the permission of BOA Editions, Ltd., 92 Park Ave., Brockport, NY 14420.

cummings, e. e.: From *Poems: 1923–1954.* Published by Harcourt Brace.

Dyer, Raymond: Reprinted with permission of *The Old Farmer's Almanac* © 1975, Yankee Publishing Inc., Dublin, NH.

Forman, Ruth: From *We Are the Young Magicians* by Ruth Forman. Copyright © 1993 by Ruth Forman. Reprinted by permission of Beacon Press, Boston.

Frost, Robert: From *The Poetry of Robert Frost* edited by Edward Connery Lathem. Copyright 1951 by Robert Frost. Copyright 1923 © 1969 by Henry Holt and Co., Inc. Reprinted by permission of Henry Holt and Co., Inc.

Gallagher, Tess: "Stubborn Kisses" copyright 1992 by Tess Gallagher. Reprinted from *Portable Kisses,* Capra Press, 1992, by permission of the author.

Hernandez, David: "Martin and My Father," "Armitage Street," and "Puerto Rice N'Beans" reprinted by permission of the author.

Hongo, Garrett: From *Yellow Light* by permission of Wesleyan University Press. © 1982 Garrett Hongo.

Knoepfle, John: "Watching a Haircut" from *Poems from the Sangamon* by John Knoepfle. © 1985 by John Knoepfle. Used with the permission of the author and the University of Illinois Press.

Lee, Li-Young: "The Gift" copyright © 1986 by Li-Young Lee. Reprinted from *Rose,* by Li-Young Lee, with the permission of BOA Editions, Ltd., 92 Park Ave., Brockport, NY 14420.

Neruda, Pablo: "Poetry" from *Selected Poems* by Pablo Neruda. Published by Random House. Reprinted with permission.

Phillips, Frank L.: Reprinted from *American Negro Poetry,* edited by Arna Bontemps.

Plath, Sylvia: All lines from "Mirror" from *Crossing the Water* by Sylvia Plath. Copyright © 1963 by Ted Hughes. Originally appeared in *The New Yorker.* Reprinted by permission of Harper Collins Publishers, Inc.

Rich, Adrienne: "Song" is reprinted from *Diving into the Wreck: Poems 1971–1972* by Adrienne Rich, by permission of the author and W. W. Norton & Company, Inc. Copyright © 1973 by W. W. Norton & Company, Inc.

Seibles, Tim: "The Good City" by Tim Seibles is reprinted with permission of the *Spoon River Poetry Review.*

Soto, Gary: From *Black Hair.* © 1985 by the University of Pittsburgh Press.

Stanford, Frank: Reprinted by permission of the University of Arkansas Press.

Stryk, Lucien: "Garage Sale" from *Of Pen and Ink and Paper Scraps,* and "Cherries" and "The Christ of Pershing Square" from *Collected Poems* by Lucien Stryk. Reprinted with the permission of Ohio University Press/ Swallow Press, Athens.

Every effort has been made to contact copyright holders. Errors and omissions will be corrected upon written notification.

Index